Activity Theory in HCI

Fundamentals and Reflections

Synthesis Lectures on Human-Centered Informatics

Editor

John M. Carroll, *Penn State University*

Human-Centered Informatics (HCI) is the intersection of the cultural, the social, the cognitive, and the aesthetic with computing and information technology. It encompasses a huge range of issues, theories, technologies, designs, tools, environments and human experiences in knowledge work, recreation and leisure activity, teaching and learning, and the potpourri of everyday life. The series will publish state-of-the-art syntheses, case studies, and tutorials in key areas. It will share the focus of leading international conferences in HCI.

Activity Theory in HCI: Fundamentals and Reflections
Victor Kaptelinin and Bonnie Nardi
2012

Conceptual Models: Core to Good Design
Jeff Johnson and Austin Henderson
2011

Geographical Design: Spatial Cognition and Geographical Information Science
Stephen C. Hirtle
2011

User-Centered Agile Methods
Hugh Beyer
2010

Experience-Centered Design: Designers, Users, and Communities in Dialogue

Peter Wright and John McCarthy
2010

Experience Design: Technology for All the Right Reasons
Marc Hassenzahl
2010

Designing and Evaluating Usable Technology in Industrial Research: Three Case Studies
Clare-Marie Karat and John Karat
2010

Interacting with Information
Ann Blandford and Simon Attfield
2010

Designing for User Engagement: Aesthetic and Attractive User Interfaces
Alistair Sutcliffe
2009

Context-Aware Mobile Computing: Affordances of Space, Social Awareness, and Social Influence
Geri Gay
2009

Studies of Work and the Workplace in HCI: Concepts and Techniques
Graham Button and Wes Sharrock
2009

Semiotic Engineering Methods for Scientific Research in HCI
Clarisse Sieckenius de Souza and Carla Faria Leitão
2009

Common Ground in Electronically Mediated Conversation
Andrew Monk
2008

Activity Theory in HCI: Fundamentals and Reflections

Victor Kaptelinin and Bonnie Nardi

ISBN: 978-3-031-01068-2   paperback
ISBN: 978-3-031-02196-1   ebook

DOI 10.1007/978-3-031-02196-1

A Publication in the Springer series
SYNTHESIS LECTURES ON HUMAN-CENTERED INFORMATICS

Lecture #13
Series Editor: John M. Carroll, *Penn State University*
Series ISSN
Synthesis Lectures on Human-Centered Informatics
Print 1946-7680   Electronic 1946-7699

Activity Theory in HCI

Fundamentals and Reflections

Victor Kaptelinin
University of Bergen and Umeå University

Bonnie Nardi
University of California, Irvine

SYNTHESIS LECTURES ON HUMAN-CENTERED INFORMATICS #13

ABSTRACT

Activity theory—a conceptual framework originally developed by Aleksei Leontiev—has its roots in the socio-cultural tradition in Russian psychology. The foundational concept of the theory is human *activity*, which is understood as purposeful, mediated, and transformative interaction between human beings and the world. Since the early 1990s, activity theory has been a visible landmark in the theoretical landscape of Human-Computer Interaction (HCI). Along with some other frameworks, such as distributed cognition and phenomenology, it established itself as a leading post-cognitivist approach in HCI and interaction design. In this book we discuss the conceptual foundations of activity theory and its contribution to HCI research. After making the case for theory in HCI and briefly discussing the contribution of activity theory to the field (Chapter 1) we introduce the historical roots, main ideas, and principles of activity theory (Chapter 2). After that we present in-depth analyses of three issues which we consider of special importance to current developments in HCI and interaction design, namely: agency (Chapter 3), experience (Chapter 4), and activity-centric computing (Chapter 5). We conclude the book with reflections on challenges and prospects for further development of activity theory in HCI (Chapter 6).

KEYWORDS

activity theory, post-cognitivist theory, object-orientedness, hierarchical structure of activity, mediation, externalization, internalization, development, activity system model, agency, experience, activity-centric computing, hn-HC

Contents

Preface

In graduate school, one of our professors once said, "Social theory should be judged according to standards of *truth, beauty, and justice*." The authors judge activity theory highly, but we recall this statement to draw attention to the burden of the professor's message which asserts that theory is a special kind of artifact embodying the highest human values. Encountering activity theory provides an opportunity not only to learn the specifics of the theory but to pause for reflections on the standards to which we hold science and design.

Truth is no easy thing. It is legitimate to be troubled by simplistic notions of truth, to believe only in partial truths, to insist on the wobbly provisionality of all knowledge. But we can still root for the truth because *in practice*, whether the quotidian empirics of everyday life or the grand labors of Nobel Prize-winning scientific research, we prefer to know rather than not to know. Truth in theory speaks to a fundamental human orientation to reality.

The beauty of theory is perhaps less apparent. Aesthetic qualities are, however, apprehended readily enough when one immerses in theory. The revelatory experiences theory permits occur as moments of altered perception when we see what we did not see before, when refigured ideas and objects educate us to understand the world more complexly. These moments move us as deeply as an artist's unique visions. The standard of beauty in theory is part of its essence as much as truth-seeking.

We puzzled over the "justice" part of the professor's statement for some years. Finally we came to see it as the most important quality of a theory of social life. This standard seems a contradiction though—perhaps the truth is not just and it would be disingenuous or delusional to pretend otherwise. But social theory inevitably weaves itself back into the practices of our lives. If we believe that man is a rational problem solver, maximizing utility, we begin to design institutions around that notion, to live as though it were true. The injustices of this view need not be retailed here (but they start with "man"). Activity theory is animated by an optimistic, positive, forward looking prospect in which imaginative reflexive activity always holds possibilities for just action. The caring notion of *development* foundational to activity theory proposed, from activity theory's earliest beginnings, that we humans are responsible for one another's development, and that growth and change continually renew our potentials as human beings. Early activity theory research concerning education for the lower classes, improved services for the disabled, and more just means of educational testing deliberately focused on areas in which important aspects of human development were at stake.

Now as we design and analyze digital technologies that affect billions of people *we* are in part responsible, through the agency of these powerful technologies, for broad swaths of the course of human development—education, social life, commerce, governance. To the extent that technologies are inflected by figurations of theory, consequential action depends on the standards of the theories we invoke.

Throughout the writing of this book it has been a pleasure to work with Jack Carroll, Series Editor, who gave us the opportunity to contribute to Morgan & Claypool's Synthesis Lectures on Human-Centered Informatics. Many thanks to Morgan & Claypool editor Diane Cerra for her flawless good sense, flexibility, enthusiasm, and guidance. We are grateful to Liam Bannon, Susanne Bødker, and Clay Spinuzzi for astute comments on earlier version of the manuscript. Errors and omissions remain our own.

Victor Kaptelinin and Bonnie Nardi
March 2012

CHAPTER 1

Introduction: Activity theory and the changing face of HCI

THEORY IN HCI

The need for theory in human-computer interaction (HCI) is not self-obvious. Much of HCI research, let alone practice, does not use any theory (at least, not explicitly). Concrete user studies, as well as design or evaluation projects, often describe the methods employed but are rarely framed within a theoretical framework.

However, a closer look reveals that theory in HCI plays a more substantial role than what skimming through journal and conference papers in the field might suggest. First, even though papers and books explicitly referring to theory—any theory—are a minority, their absolute number is not insignificant. Table 1.1 shows the number of hits produced by using the names of selected theoretical frameworks as search strings in the ACM Digital Library. The figures suggest that hundreds of studies are employing theory, one way or another. Second, and more importantly, while not statistically prevalent, theoretical and theory-informed explorations in HCI have greatly contributed to the shaping of the field as a whole.

The very emergence of HCI as a field of research should be credited to adopting the information processing psychology perspective on human interaction with technology (Card et al., 1983). Information processing psychology contributed to the development of the field in a variety of ways. It served as a cross-disciplinary matchmaker by bringing together psychologists interested in computer technology and computer scientists interested in user interfaces and user behavior. It provided a common language that could be used by people with different disciplinary backgrounds. And it was instrumental in defining the agenda of early HCI, with its focus on formal (or semiformal) interaction models and controlled experiments.

Around the late 1980s–early 1990s, when HCI was reinventing itself as a field dealing with "human actors" rather than "human factors" (Bannon, 1991), theoretical considerations were also of central importance. The shift from the "first wave HCI" to the "second wave HCI" (Cooper and Bowers, 1995) was motivated by the need to overcome the limitations of information processing psychology as a theoretical foundation for HCI (Carroll, 1991). A variety of theoretical approaches were proposed as alternative frameworks for the second wave HCI (Kaptelinin et al., 2003). They included, among others, phenomenology (Winograd and Flores, 1987), the situated action perspective (Suchman, 1987), activity theory (Bødker, 1991), and distributed cognition (Hollan et al., 2000; Norman, 1991). These frameworks contributed to extending the scope of HCI and prioritizing understanding and supporting meaningful human action and social interaction in everyday contexts.

Table 1.1: Second wave theories: Number of hits in ACM Digital Library (www.dl.acm.org) on March 7, 2012.

Search string	Number of hits	Search string	Number of hits
phenomenology	1635	phenomenology & HCI	261
"activity theory"	1578	"activity theory" & HCI	533
"distributed cognition"	1156	"distributed cognition" & HCI	401
ethnomethodology	642	ethnomethodology & HCI	277
"situated action"	571	"situated action" & HCI	213
"language action"	468	"language action" & HCI	68
"actor network theory"	399	"actor network theory" & HCI	47
"external cognition"	146	"external cognition" & HCI	62

Activity theory, a conceptual approach originating in the Russian psychology of the 1920s and 1930s, maintains that human uses of technology can only be understood in the context of purposeful, mediated, and developing interaction between active "subjects" and the world (that is, "objects"). The theory was one of the leading contenders as a theoretical foundation for second-wave HCI. Along with other frameworks, activity theory has contributed to the conceptual transformation of HCI in the 1990s and has established itself as a key element of HCI's current theoretical landscape. Carroll (2011) observed that "the most canonical theory-base in HCI now is sociocultural, Activity Theory." In discussing how "the features of particular artifacts become entangled in the social practices of people's work," Leonardi and Barley (2008) note that "students of computer-supported cooperative work whose work is rooted in ethnomethodology and activity theory have made the most progress on this score."

THE OBJECTIVES OF THE BOOK

The most immediate aim of this book is to introduce the basic principles of activity theory and discuss key applications in HCI, with a special focus on recent HCI research. After briefly outlining the main types of contributions of the theory to the field we provide a concise exposition of the principles of activity theory. Then we move to a discussion of three key topical areas for HCI: agency, experience, and activity-centric computing. Finally, we discuss new streams of research in HCI such as sustainable interaction design, ICTD, and collapse computing. We suggest the relevance of activity theory to these emergent paradigms.

More broadly, we want to argue for the importance of nuanced explanation and interpretation in HCI—goals that are well served by theory. While practical concerns such as product usability are of critical importance, the ultimate purpose of research is, as Kuutti (2010) remarks, "to develop better understanding of the world around us." Research is a human quest of much larger scope than a particular invention or corporate need or user experience. Kuuti (2010) makes the case nicely: "If we focus only on practical usefulness and exclude explanation and interpretation, we do serious harm to our very nature as researchers."

The journey to theory may be long and arduous. But we believe that those of us who understand technology—which we regard as the most powerfully shaping force of our era—have a special brief to be aware of and to engage theories that underwrite certain intellectual and ethical commitments. While we realize that not everyone heeds this call, the commitments are of significant social importance and include: the possibility for positive change, a complexly developed notion of human agency, and the active promotion of social justice. The human-computer interaction community, while diverse and at times contentious, agrees on one thing that, within the scope of our discipline, makes these commitments tenable: technology is an outcome of design, and design is under the aegis of human intentionality and imagination. The logic of this simple statement is profoundly empowering. As human beings, we have the capacity to shape our own futures.

As agreeable as this logic probably is to most in the HCI community, beyond our community not everyone sees it quite this way. Activity theorist Anna Stetsenko (2008) offers a cautionary tale on the current state of social theory and its wider societal implications. Despite technology's ascendance —which would suggest theoretical emphasis on human creativity and agency—Stetsenko points to the regressive, sociobiologically-oriented theory that dominates much current discourse:

[We see] a rising tide, indeed a tsunami, of starkly mechanistic views that reduce human development (more boldly now than at any other time in recent history) to processes in the brain rigidly constrained by genetic blueprints passed on to contemporary humans from the dawn of evolution. [T]hese views . . . draw together resurrected tenets of sociobiology, innatist linguistics, narrowly conceived neuroscience, orthodox modular cognitivism, with [notions of] test-and-control knowledge transmission.

Many of us in HCI would wonder how rigid blueprints begat Google, Facebook, Twitter, YouTube, Wikipedia, virtual worlds, massively multiplayer video games with millions of participants, and the other highly imaginative technologies that are part of our lives—all of which came into being within living memory of most inhabitants of the planet. What mechanistic, genetic explanation harking back to the dawn of evolution could foster inquiry into these technologies and our relations to them? As readily as we might reject genetically based explanations, we ourselves have not taken the crucial step of theorizing these unprecedented sociotechnical developments. We ignore theory, and the very act of theorizing, at our peril. Stetsenko (2008) notes that sociocultural approaches —"critical pedagogy, social theory, adult learning, disability studies, critical race theory, constructivist education, science studies, human-computer interaction, feminist studies, literary criticism, cultural anthropology, and developmental psychology"—are a looser and less powerful coalition than the theories that comprise the "reductionist synthesis."

The mechanistic view has badly overshadowed socially inflected theorizing. There seem to be two reasons. First, sociocultural approaches are "disconnected, without much dialogue or coordination among them" (Stetsenko, 2008). Second, many (though not all) sociocultural approaches produce that vacuum nature abhors—into which reductionist theory rushes. Skepticism about "grand theory" coupled with a penchant for detailed, literarily modulated but undertheorized discussions of cultural constructions, fragmented identities, decentered selves, and so on, cede control to reductionist theory with its clear, bold articulation of what it means to be human. However well-deserved postmodern critiques of inflexible standards of truth may be, their fatal flaw is to leave nothing when people want something. Stetsenko's (2008) eloquent statement is a touchstone for why theory matters:

[M]any scholars of culture today are interested in addressing complexity and fluidity of identity and subjectivity by focusing on their permeable boundaries and fleeting expressions—their grounding in dispersed networks and multilayered sites—and are less interested in explicitly conceptualizing human development and nature, including the broadest question of what it means to be human. However, these "big" questions do not and will not go away. When they remain undertheorized, the door is left open for essentialist premises to sneak right back into even the utmost critical and cultural conceptions of human development . . . (Stetsenko, 2008)

While many of us in the academy (including both of us) hesitate over totalizing discourses, univocal treatments, and simplistic positivism, our finely tuned sensitivities are at risk of devolving into something merely precious, losing sight of broader objectives and societal goals. If we refuse the call to answer the big questions, they will be answered by others whose answers we might not like very much.

Academic accounts inevitably bleed into popular media, political discourse, and policy discussions. Stetsenko (2008) argues that "Given the recent tidal wave of simplified reductionist notions about human nature and development . . . the goal of developing an alternative broad vision appears to be not only important but urgently needed." With Stetsenko, we believe that activity theory has an important place in theorizing an alternative vision to the big questions. Activity theory keeps these questions front and center. What does it mean to be human? How are mind and consciousness related? What is the nature of human action? We can dismiss these questions as tired remnants of grand theory, but the questions never fail to reassert themselves.

ACTIVITY THEORY IN HCI: SELECTED CONTRIBUTIONS

Before proceeding to the next chapter which addresses basic principles of activity theory, we try to set the scene by discussing how activity theory is being used within the field of human-computer interaction[1]. Since its introduction to the field in the late 1980s (Bødker, 1989), activity theory has been applied in a wide range of studies. Early applications of activity theory were predominantly either: (a) making the case for the theory as a theoretical foundation for the field; or (b) retrospective analyses of previous research or development projects. Applications of the first type including the pioneering work of Bødker (1989; 1991), as well as other early theoretical explorations, such as those by Kuutti (1991), Nardi (1992), and Kaptelinin (1992), employed activity theory as a conceptual *orienting framework* for HCI—a framework that was expected to provide a logically consistent view of the field as a whole and help formulate new relevant research questions. Applications of the second type, retrospective analyses (e.g., Bødker, 1991; Nardi, 1994), employed the theory as a *theoretical lens*, that is, a conceptual tool to help analyze concrete empirical evidence by highlighting key issues for detailed examination and suggesting possible interpretations.

In the last two decades the ways of using the theory have changed in several respects. First, the aim of applying activity theory as a conceptual orienting basis is no longer to make a general case for activity theory as a theoretical foundation of HCI. Theoretical explorations have become more concrete and differentiated, focusing on either specific areas of study, such as mobile learning (Uden, 2007) and design research (Kuutti, 2010), or specific HCI concepts, such as affordances (Albrechtsen et al., 2001; Baerentsen and Trettvik, 2002; Kaptelinin and Nardi, 2012) or services (Kaptelinin and Uden, 2012).

Second, a similar trend toward more concrete and differentiated uses of the theory is evident when considering the theory employed as a theoretical lens. Not only is activity theory being used now within ongoing projects (rather than retrospectively), it is also employed in more nuanced ways, capitalizing on a wider and more articulated set of concepts (e.g., Bødker and Andersen, 2005; Manker and Arvola, 2011; Nardi, 2005).

Third, applications of the theory have been progressively more focused on design. Even though in HCI there is a fine line between analysis and design, one can still differentiate between research which is mostly concerned with understanding people, and research which is mostly concerned with exploring novel ways of supporting people with interactive technologies. The contribution of activity theory to the latter has been twofold. On the one hand, the theory stimulated the development of a variety of analytical tools for design and evaluation. On the other hand, its applications resulted in a number of novel systems, implementing the ideas of activity-centric (or activity-based) computing.

In general, activity theory contributions to the field of HCI have been of the following three types: (a) theoretical re-framing of some of the most basic HCI concepts, (b) providing conceptual tools for design and evaluation, and (c) serving as a theoretical lens in empirical studies. Let us consider a few selected examples.

RE-FRAMING HCI CONCEPTS

The unit of analysis proposed by activity theory, that is, "subject-object" interaction, may appear similar to the traditional focus of HCI on "human-computer" interaction. However, adopting an activity theoretical perspective has had important implications for understanding how people use interactive technologies. First of all, it made immediately obvious that "computer" is typically not an object of activity but rather a mediating artifact. Therefore, generally speaking, people are not interacting *with* computers: they interact with the world *through* computers. The book by Susanne Bødker which played a key role in introducing activity theory to HCI reflected this perspective on interactive technologies in its title: *Through the Interface: An Activity-theoretical Perspective on Human-computer Interaction* (Bødker, 1991).

Another general theoretical contribution of activity theory to HCI was placing computer use in the hierarchical structure of human activity, that is, relating the operational (low-level) aspects of interaction with technology to meaningful goals and, ultimately, the needs and motives of technology users. It did not mean rejecting the formal models of users and tasks developed in early HCI research, but rather called for extending the scope of analysis beyond low-level interaction to the higher level concerns of motivation and goal seeking. Such an extension is consistent with the need of the field to move "from human factors to human actors" (Bannon, 1991).

In our recent paper (Kaptelinin and Nardi, 2012) we employ activity theory to reappraise the notion of affordance in HCI. We argue that the original Gibsonian notion (Gibson, 1979) is of limited relevance to the field because it predominantly focuses on "animal-environment" interaction and fails to recognize technologies as culturally developed tools mediating human interaction with the world. We concur with Gibson that a natural human way to perceive the environment is to actively pick up information about possibilities for action, that is, affordances. However, we understand technology as a mediational means employed in social, cultural environments, which has direct implications for how technology affordances are conceptualized. In particular, we argue that action possibilities provided by a technology comprise two related facets: (a) possibilities for interacting *with* the technology (P-T), i.e., *handling affordances*, and (b) possibilities for employing the technology to make an effect on an object (T-O), i.e., *effecter* affordances. Together, they define instrumental technology affordances as possibilities for acting *through* the technology in question on a certain object ((P-T)-O).

CONCEPTUAL TOOLS FOR DESIGN AND EVALUATION

Activity theory is a clarifying, orienting framework. It is not a "theory" in the traditional sense in which theory is understood in natural sciences. Activity theory does not support creating and running predictive models which only need be "fed" with appropriate data. Instead, it aims to help researchers and practitioners orientate themselves in complex real-life problems, identify key issues that need to be dealt with, and direct the search for relevant evidence and suitable solutions. In other words, the key advantage of activity theory is to support researchers and practitioners in their own inquiry—for instance, by helping to ask right questions—rather than providing ready-made answers.

Activity theory has spawned a number of practical tools for design and evaluation. These tools support asking "the right questions" in the analysis, design, and evaluation of interactive systems (Quek and Shah, 2004). Many such tools have the format of a checklist: they are, essentially, organized lists of questions or issues that researchers or practitioners need to pay attention to in order to make sure that the most important aspects of human activity are taken into account.

The choice of the checklist format is intended to help bridge the gap between theory's high level of abstraction and the need to address concrete issues in analysis and design. Activity theory is a high level framework, not limited to particular types of artifacts, and needs to be adjusted to HCI research and practice. Activity theory-based checklists reduce the effort associated with domain-specific adjustment of the theory by converting the organized set of concepts, offered by the theory, into a set of concrete issues and questions, directly related to analysis and design of interactive technologies.

Different checklists are based on different variants of activity theory. For instance, the Activity Checklist (Kaptelinin et al., 1999) is intended to support systematic exploration of the "space of context" in design and evaluation of interactive technologies. The overall structure of the checklist is derived from the basic principles of Leontiev's framework and comprises four sections—Means and ends; The environment; Learning; cognition, and articulation; and Development. The checklist was employed in a number of design and evaluation projects (see Kaptelinin and Nardi, 2006). In a recent study by Manker and Arvola (2011) the Activity Checklist was employed as a tool for structuring and interpretation of empirical evidence collected in an interview study of prototyping in game design.

Jonassen and Rohrer-Murphy (1999) introduce another analytical tool based on a somewhat different (while partly overlapping) set of activity-theoretical concepts. The tool comprises several organized arrays of questions and issues derived from Engeström's activity system model (discussed in detail in the next chapter). The basic components of the model —Subject, Object, and Community, as well as Tools, Rules, and Roles mediating the three-way interaction between the components—serve as the rubric for issues that need to be taken into account and modeled when designing the components of a constructivist learning environment and relationships between the components. Mwanza's AODM (Activity-oriented design method) approach to supporting technology-enhanced learning analysis and design includes lists of issues to explore (Mwanza, 2002). The AODM capitalizes on the conceptual structure provided by Engeström's activity system model.

Matthews et al. (2007) developed a framework, informed by activity theory, for understanding, designing, and evaluating peripheral displays. The framework employs the activity-theoretical distinction between conscious actions and automatic operations to define the notion of "peripheral displays" which are primarily used at the operation level. In addition, the framework introduces a useful taxonomy of activities depending on their current status: (a) primary (foreground) activities, (b) secondary (background) activities, (c) pending activities, which are likely to become primary ones, and (d) dormant activities. The authors propose a set of evaluation criteria and a list of design guidelines for designing and evaluating peripheral displays.

Li and Landay (2008) report the design, implementation, and testing of the ActivityDesigner, a design environment for prototyping ubiquitous computing applications to support everyday activities that take place over extended periods. The ActivityDesigner allows designers to integrate field observations, activity analysis and modeling, interaction prototyping, and *in situ* testing within the overall framework of an Activity-Based Ubicomp Prototyping process.

Bødker and Klokmose (2011) propose the Human-Artifact Model, a minimalist activity-theory based representation of various aspects of an artifact combined with corresponding levels of human activity, intended to be used in analysis and design of interactive artifacts with little or no prior knowledge of activity theory. The model is argued to be a powerful tool for providing an account of action possibilities offered by an artifact as contextualized in larger-scale "ecologies of artifacts."

THEORETICAL LENS

One of the most common ways of applying activity theory in HCI is using its concepts when analyzing empirical evidence obtained in a study. Bryant et al. (2005) interviewed expert contributors to Wikipedia and used Engeström's activity system model as a conceptual tool for understanding the development of novices into "Wikipedians." The authors showed that the development can be described in terms of the transformation of subjects, transformation of tool use (e.g., the use of editing tools and watchlists), as well as transformation of subjects' perceptions of community, rules, and division of labor.

Empirical studies of collaboration conducted by Carroll and his colleagues (Carroll et al., 2006; Carroll, 2012) suggest that in real-life contexts the phenomena of awareness—one of the key objects of study in CSCW research—include more than merely awareness in respect to joint actions, mutual presence, and shared situations. Carroll observes:

In framing activity awareness, we appropriated the concept of activity from Activity Theory, to emphasize that collaborators need be aware of a whole, shared activity as complex, socially and culturally embedded endeavor, organized in dynamic hierarchies, and not merely aware of the synchronous and easily noticeable aspects of the activity (Carroll, 2012).

SOME REFLECTIONS FOR STUDENTS

We take a moment to address a few words primarily to students. In this era of mashups, machinimas, markups, and other combinations-and-permutations derivatives, the craft of theorizing may give way to less demanding "one from column A and one from column B" approaches. (We recently reviewed a paper which invoked actor-network theory, activity theory, performativity, sociomateriality, the mangle of practice, processes of imbrication, and agential cuts.) Unruly theoretical mixing and matching risks illogic and inconsistency. A theory has integrity; it constitutes a set of commitments. A theory contains axioms, principles, and perspectives. It defines and delineates a world view. Theory is accountable to its principles: it states and defends claims. In the logic of a theory, concepts build on and articulate with one another. Analysis by lazy bricolage—tossing in one theoretical bit here, another there—is probably going to end in an incoherent mess.

In making this argument, we are not eschewing principled theoretical synthesis. Far from it. Often the way forward is by means of artful theoretical melds—theories can and should mutually inform and influence one another. But we must also be alert to the conceptual spaces in which theories conflict and diverge. It is here that we sometimes fail to apprehend what it is a theory is standing up for, its non-negotiable demands. To deal with this complexity, we suggest taking time to internalize a few theories from the bottom up, to appreciate the commitments and logics they entail. We hope this book will be a means for finding an appreciation of activity theory. Even if readers do not ultimately choose activity theory for their research, there is pedagogical value in taking activity theory as a "worked example" of fundamental concepts of subject and object, history, development, mediation, and so on. Examining how activity theory presents and articulates such concepts repays study. It will be clearer how, by contrast, other theories deal with these concepts. Or how they do not deal with them at all.

Theory is a tool for thinking. As with any tool, knowing what it is capable of, how it works, its capacities and limitations, are essential for effective use. We believe that in reaching an appreciation of theory, readers will find, at a minimum, the reward of the aesthetics of good theory. Within a good theory, concepts flow into and affirm one another, a distinctive picture of reality is rendered, things unseen are now seen.

The converse is, of course, also true. Theories cast shadows, they leave areas of darkness. Discerning these shadows can inspire us to produce new theory. In Chapter 6, for example, we draw on Bødker and Andersen's discussion of complex mediation that interweaves activity theory and semiotic analysis (see also González et al., 2009; Rogers, 2004; Stahl, 2011 for extensions to theory). As tools, theories are mutable things that can be refined, reshaped, recast, reimagined. They are wonderful, even amazing, products of human imagination. Given our enthusiasm for theory, it is no surprise that we hope that engaging activity theory will lead you to appreciate the beautiful logics and intuitions of a well-crafted theory, whatever theory it may be.

The book is organized as follows. Chapter 2 provides an introduction to activity theory, its historical roots, main ideas, and principles. The next chapters go into depth on the concepts of agency and "experience," and then activity-centric computing. Chapter 6 concludes with reflections on current applications of activity theory in HCI, as well as challenges and opportunities for future development of the theory.

[1]We do not aim to provide a representative overview of HCI and interaction design research informed by activity theory. Such overviews can be found elsewhere (see, for instance, Bertelsen and Bødker, 2003; Kaptelinin and Nardi, 2006; Nardi, 1996a,b, and Wilson, 2008).

CHAPTER 2

Basic concepts and principles of activity theory

INTRODUCTION

Since early work in HCI and activity theory such as Bødker (1989) and Nardi (1996a), "activity" has entered the HCI conversation as researchers attempt to reformulate study in more expansive ways sensitive to the realities of our lives. As Moran (2005a) noted, "Activity is a central theoretical construct in HCI/CSCW research and theory." This welcome development demonstrates a serious commitment to apprehending the complexity of human life as a necessary research strategy in HCI.

However, it is often the case that even within more expansive approaches, "activity" is undertheorized. It is used primarily in an intuitive or common sense way. Activity theory goes beyond commonsense/intuitive notions of activity and takes a close look at what activity can mean in more precise, theoretically informed ways. In this chapter we examine how activity theory conceives activity.

We present an introduction to activity theory, its basic concepts and principles. We start with a discussion of the notion of activity as a psychological concept as it was developed in Russian psychology of the early 20th century, and reflect on the historical roots of activity theory. Then we give an overview of the underlying ideas and principles of the activity theoretical approach developed by Alexey Leontiev (1978; 1981), and, finally, describe the version of activity theory, based on Leontiev's approach, which was proposed by Yrjö Engeström (Engeström, 1987; Engeström et al., 1999).

A few clarifications are in order before we proceed further. First, this introduction reflects our own attempt to discern and organize the underlying ideas of activity theory, which are seldom presented in a concise and structured way in the original texts by Leontiev and other scholars who contributed to the development of the approach. Other interpretations of the basic concepts and principles of activity theory can also be found in the literature. While these interpretations are largely consistent with one another, they may differ in certain details.

Second, this chapter specifically deals with two versions of activity theory: the approach developed by Leontiev and a closely related approach proposed by Engeström. By "activity theory" in general we mean an aggregated framework comprising a combination of these two approaches. There are other approaches, which have "activity theory" in their names, as well. A systematic exploration of the question of what (if any) conceptual links are there between these approaches and the ones developed by Leontiev and Engeström is beyond the scope of our discussion here.

Third, various transliterations of the Russian last name "Леонтьев" are found in the literature. In addition to "Leontiev," the spellings employed include "Leont'ev," "Leontjew," and so forth. To avoid possible confusion, we uniformly use "Leontiev" throughout the book. Alternative spellings are additionally indicated in the reference list, when appropriate.

THE GENERAL NOTION OF ACTIVITY

"Activity," the foundational concept of activity theory, is understood as a relationship between the subject (that is, an actor) and the object (that is, an entity objectively existing in the world). A common way to represent activity is "S < − > O."

The concept refers to a special type of relationship between the subject and the object; it is characterized by two distinctive features: (a) subjects of activities have needs, which should be met through subjects' interaction with the world, and (b) activities and the entities they are relating (i.e., subjects and objects) mutually determine one another. More generally, activities are generative forces that transform both subjects and objects.

Subjects have needs. Activity is understood as a "unit of life" of a material subject existing in the objective world. Subjects have their own needs and, in order to survive, must carry out activities, that is, interact with objects of the world to meet the needs. Leontiev's analysis was mostly concerned with activities of individual human beings, but the notion of "subject" is not limited to individual humans. Other types of entities, such as animals, teams, and organizations can also have need-based agency and, therefore, be subjects of activities (Kaptelinin and Nardi, 2006).

Activities and their subjects mutually determine one another. It is immediately obvious that activities are influenced by the attributes of subjects and objects. Consider a simple example. Undoubtedly, whether or not a person can solve a math problem depends on the nature of the problem (e.g., how difficult it is) and the person's abilities and skills (i.e., how good the person is at math). In the long run, however, the opposite is also true: both the object and the subject are over time transformed by the activity. It is apparent, for instance, that a person's math skills are a result of previous experience: they have developed through solving math problems in the past. In other words, while a person's math abilities determine how the person solves math problems, it is also true that solving math problems determine the person's math abilities. Therefore, subjects do not only express themselves in their activities; in a very real sense they are produced by the activities (cf. Rubinshtein, 1986).

This view of human activity is a hallmark of an age-old intellectual tradition that manifested itself throughout history in a variety of seemingly diverse schools of thought, one way or another. This view emphasizes the fundamental inseparability of human beings and the world, as well as the generative and transformative nature of purposeful human action. Some of the early insights stemming from the tradition can be found in Eastern philosophy, most notably Buddhism. Buddha is believed to teach, for instance, that:

One is not a Brahmin by birth,

Nor by birth a non-Brahmin.

By action is one a Brahmin,

By action is one a non-Brahmin.

So that is how the truly wise

See action as it really is.

Seers of dependent origination,

Skilled in actions and its results.

Action makes the world go round

Action makes this generation turn.

Living beings are bound by action

Like the chariot wheel by the pin.

Despite their differences, both activity theory and Buddhism consider the contradistinction between the subject and the object as something that is not inherently given but rather produced by action.

In Western thought the fundamental insight of the inseparability of subjects and objects is expressed, for instance, in the philosophical views of Hegel and Marx, Goethe's poetry, Brentano's "act psychology," and the ecological psychology of Gibson.

THE ORIGINS OF ACTIVITY THEORY: RUSSIAN PSYCHOLOGY OF THE 1920s AND 1930s

The immediate conceptual origins of activity theory can be found in Russian/Soviet psychology of the 1920s and 1930s. During that time theoretical explorations in Russian psychology were heavily influenced by Marxist philosophy. A collective effort of a number of prominent Soviet psychologists, most notably Lev Vygotsky and Sergei Rubinshtein—an effort that also involved much disagreement and even open conflicts—gave rise to a broadly understood sociocultural perspective in Russian psychology.

The main conceptual thrust of the sociocultural perspective was to overcome the divide between, on the one hand, human mind, and on the other hand, culture and society. As opposed to most psychological frameworks of that time, the perspective considered culture and society generative forces, "responsible" for the very production of human mind, rather than external factors, however important, that constitute conditions for the functioning of mind without changing its basic nature.

The work based on the sociocultural perspective produced a number of fundamental insights. Some of the most important contributions were as follows:

- Vygotsky's (1978) universal law of development, according to which human mental functions first emerge as distributed between the person and other people (i.e., as "inter-psychological" ones) and only then as individually mastered by the person himself or herself (i.e., as "intra-psychological" ones), and

- The principle of "unity and inseparability of consciousness and activity," proposed by Rubinshtein (1946) according to which human conscious experience and human acting in the world, the internal and the external, are closely interconnected and mutually determine one another.

Leontiev's activity theory[2] emerged as an outgrowth of the sociocultural perspective. The theory employs a number of ideas developed by Vygotsky, Leontiev's mentor and friend. It is also strongly influenced by the work of Rubinshtein, a major figure in Russian psychology and a long-time colleague of Leontiev's (Brushlinsky and Aboulhanova-Slavskaya, 2000). Arguably, activity theory also features some other influences which are more difficult to discern, such as the framework developed by Mikhail Basov (1991). The basic assumptions of activity theory are the same as those underlying the sociocultural perspective in Russian psychology in general: namely, the assumptions of the social nature of human mind and inseparability of human mind and activity.

At the same time, Leontiev's activity theory was not a simple imprint of all these influences. As discussed below, while the framework incorporates a variety of ideas developed by Vygotsky, Rubinshstein, and others, these ideas were revised and elaborated upon by Leontiev to form his own distinct and consistent conceptual framework.

LEV VYGOTSKY AND THE SOCIAL NATURE OF HUMAN MIND

The most fundamental issue for Vygotsky was the relationship between the mind, on the one hand, and culture and society, on the other. He maintained that culture and society are not merely external factors influencing the mind but rather generative forces directly involved in the very production of mind. It was critically important, according to Vygotsky, that this fundamental idea be assimilated by psychology.

The clear implication of this postulate is that our relation to technology (which is part of culture) is a deep one; the use of technology materially shapes who we are and become. Technologies do not exist simply as neutral "helpers" "out there" that we pick and choose from according to the demands of some task. We grow and change in intimate relation to and with technology, developing as skilled persons according to how we learn and use technology. Our very personality and identity spring from connectedness to technology; for example, we become proficient software developers, competitive video gamers, famous bloggers. From this connection to technology, communities of practice and social networks are defined as we encounter others through the development of technologically based skills.

At the same time, Vygotsky rejected a straightforward view of culture and society as directly determining or shaping the human mind. Vygotsky argued that the only way to reveal the impact of culture on the mind was to follow developmental, historical transformations of mental phenomena in the social and cultural context. This directive is enormously challenging to execute in practice but remains an important ideal as it is seemingly the only way to confront the actual complexity of mind.

A concept proposed by Vygotsky for analysis of the social determination of mind was the notion of *higher psychological functions*. Higher psychological functions can be contrasted to "natural" psychological functions, i.e., mental abilities such as memory or perception with which every animal is born. These functions can develop as a result of maturation, practice, or imitation, but their structure does not change and these functions are basically the same in similar species. Human beings have natural psychological functions, too, which are similar to those of other primates. However, human beings also develop higher psychological functions. Higher psychological functions emerge as a result of a re-structuring of natural psychological functions in a cultural environment. This re-structuring can be described as an emerging mediation of natural psychological functions.

Human beings seldom interact with the world directly. An enormous number of artifacts has been developed by humankind to mediate our relationship with the world. Using these artifacts is the hallmark of living the life of a human being. Tools or instruments—physical artifacts mediating external activities—are easy to recognize and their impact on the everyday life of every individual is obvious.

By way of analogy to conventional technical tools (like hammers), Vygotsky introduced the notion of psychological tools, such as an algebraic notation, a map, or a blueprint. Technical tools are intended to help people affect things, while psychological tools are signs intended to help people affect others or themselves (Vygotsky, 1982). Of course, "psychological tools" and tools in a more traditional sense are very different. Vygotsky warned against pushing the analogy too far (Vygotsky, 1982, 1983)[3]. However, one thing is common to instruments and signs, which is their role in human activity. Both hammers and maps are mediators. The use of mediators, whether crushing a nutshell or becoming oriented in an unfamiliar city, changes the structure of human behavior and mental processes. Psychological tools transform natural mental processes into instrumental acts (Figure 2.1), that is, mental processes mediated by culturally developed means. Vygotsky referred to mediated mental processes as higher mental functions, to separate them from unmediated natural mental functions that can be observed in other animals as well.

Initially Vygotsky (1982) did not make a distinction between psychological tools as physical artifacts (e.g., pieces of art, maps, diagrams, blueprints) and as symbolic systems (e.g., languages, numeric systems, algebraic notations) that in some cases can exist only "in the head." It did not take long, however, for him to realize the importance of whether or not psychological tools are physical, external artifacts. Empirical studies of higher psychological functions showed that in many cases, subjects who used external mediational artifacts to solve a task spontaneously stopped using these artifacts and improved their performance. Vygotsky (1983) explained this phenomenon in terms of internalization (which he also referred to as "growing inside," *vraschivanie*, especially in his earlier works), that is, the "transition of an external operation into an internal one" (Vygotsky, 1983, our translation).

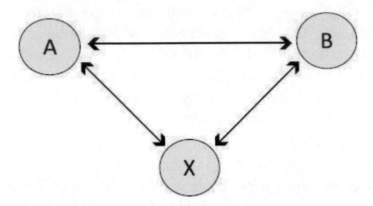

Figure 2.1: The structure of an instrumental act, based on Vygotsky (1982). "A-B" represents a simple association between two stimuli, underlying a natural mnemonic act. When memory transforms into a high-level psychological function, this association is replaced with an instrumental act comprising "A-X" and "X-B."

In the process of internalization, some of the previously external processes can take place in the internal plane, "in the head." The processes remain to be mediated, but mediated by internal signs rather than external ones. It should be emphasized that internalization is not a translation of initially external processes into a pre-existing internal plane; the internal plane itself is created through internalization (Leontiev, 1978). Internalization of mediated external processes results in mediated internal processes. Externally mediated functions become internally mediated.

Internalization is not just an elimination of external processes but rather a re-distribution of internal and external components within a function as a whole. Such a re-distribution may result in a substantial transformation of both external and internal components, such as an increased reliance on internal components at the expense of external ones, but both internal and external components are always present. The raison d'etre for internal activities is their actual or potential impact on how the individual is interacting with the world. The impact can only be made through external activities. For instance, after conducting calculations "in the head" a child may decide to buy fewer candies than she originally planned because she realizes that their total cost would exceed the amount of cash she has[4].

Over the course of internalization, external processes can transform into internal ones. There is no firm boundary between the internal, the inner world of subjective phenomena, and the external, objective world. Internalization is one of the main modes of cultural determination of the mind. Internalization enables external mediation by culturally developed tools to effect internal, mental processes, which become culturally mediated, as well.

THE INDIVIDUAL/COLLECTIVE DIMENSION: THE DYNAMICS OF THE SOCIAL DISTRIBUTION OF THE MIND

Vygotsky's call for a revision of the traditional view of a border separating the mind and the physical world was paralleled by a call for a revision of another dichotomy, the one between the individual and other people. It was claimed that individuals and their social environments are not separated by an impenetrable border. Instead, they were understood as two poles of a single dimension, which is also a dimension of the dynamics of mental processes over the course of their development.

Sometimes this dimension is not clearly differentiated from the previous one: both the internal/external dimension and the individual/collective dimension are considered different aspects of the same phenomenon of internalization. In other words, internalization is considered a process during which phenomena external to the subject, both physical and social, become both individual and internal.

However, these two dimensions—internal/external and individual/social—should not be merged into a single dimension (see also Arievitch and van der Veer, 1995). The dynamics of the internal and external components of psychological functions can be relatively independent of the dynamics of individual and collective processes.

This can be illustrated with examples of internalization that are not paralleled by a transformation of collective activities into individual ones. For instance, consider a person driving a car who initially relies on a map but eventually learns the map and gets by without it. The means of carrying out the navigation task undergoes a significant transformation: from relying on an external artifact to relying on an internalized representation. However, over the course of this transformation the activity does not necessarily become less (or more) collective; it remains an individual activity. Or let us take an example of a musician who plays in an orchestra and internalizes musical scores when participating in the collective activity. The degree to which the musician relies on external artifacts (music sheets) has little to do with participation in the collective activity of the orchestra.

These examples indicate that a decreased reliance on an external artifact does not necessarily imply a corresponding transformation of a collective activity into an individual one. It does not mean that these two dimensions are completely independent, either. They may well be two aspects of the same phenomenon. Yet they are different issues and each deserves a special analysis.

The dynamics of the individual and the social was a key issue in cultural-historical psychology. This issue was addressed by Vygotsky with two concepts, closely related to each other: the law of psychological development and the zone of proximal development.

FROM INTER-PSYCHOLOGICAL TO INTRA-PSYCHOLOGICAL

According to Vygotsky, acquisition of psychological functions is subordinated to a universal law of psychological development: new psychological functions do not directly appear as functions of the individual (i.e., intra-psychological functions). First a function is distributed between the individual and other people; it emerges as an inter-psychological function. Even though the individual may carry out some or even most components of a function, she cannot initially perform the function alone. Over time, the individual progressively masters the function and can reach the phase at which the function can be performed without help from others.

For instance, when new drivers start learning to drive a car in a specially equipped training car, they may appear responsible for the driving (since they carry out basic operations such as pressing pedals and turning the steering wheel). But much of the driving may in fact be done by the instructor, who sets the direction, monitors the overall situation, and makes most decisions. With time, the learner can assume responsibility for more and more tasks and eventually develop the ability to drive on his own. The same or similar phenomena can be observed in practically any other case of an individual acquiring a new function, including reading and writing. Even if an individual appears to learn alone, a closer look may reveal support provided by other people in the design of a textbook, the functionality of an interactive help system, or other artifacts and environments that embody the experience of other learners, helpers, and teachers.

Therefore, the "universal law of psychological development" states that new psychological functions first emerge as *inter-psychological* ones and then as *intra-psychological* ones. An application of this law to the practical tasks of assessment and support of child development resulted in the formulation of the most well-known concept of cultural historical psychology, the concept of "the zone of proximal development." The concept was defined by Vygotsky as follows:

The distance between the actual level of development as determined by independent problem solving and the level of potential development as determined through problem solving under adult guidance or in collaboration with more capable peers. (Vygotsky, 1978)

Vygotskey's suggestion was, essentially, to measure the level of development not through measuring the level of current performance, but through measuring the difference ("the distance") between two performance indicators: (1) an indicator of independent problem solving, and (2) an indicator of problem solving in a situation in which the individual is provided with support form other people.

Taken together, Vygotsky's ideas defined a new perspective in psychology, which attempted to find the origins of mind in culture and society. Many other approaches took (and still are taking) for granted that the subjective processes of the individual constitute a separate world related to objective reality mostly through perception, and it is up to the individual to decipher sensory inputs and transform them into a meaningful picture of reality. Cultural-historical psychology takes a radically difference stance. It postulates that reality itself is filled with meanings and values. Human beings develop their own meanings and values not by processing sensory inputs but by appropriating the meaning and values objectively existing in the world. The most thorough perceptual analyses of the shape, color, and other visual attributes of religious symbols and texts do not guarantee that a person understands the commandments of a religion. Such an understanding requires an interaction with the world at a higher level than visual perception: the person needs to relate to meanings that are already there. The border between the mind and the physical world, between the individual and other people, is not closed. It is being dynamically re-defined on a moment-to-moment basis depending on a variety of factors. Meaning and values can cross these borders—of course, being creatively transformed along the way.

SERGEI RUBINSHTEIN AND THE PRINCIPLE OF UNITY AND INSEPARABILITY OF CONSCIOUSNESS AND ACTIVITY

As mentioned, Leontiev's theoretical explorations of activity as a foundational concept of psychological analysis were heavily influenced by the work of Sergei Rubinshstein, and especially the principle of "unity and inseparability of consciousness and activity," proposed by Rubinshtein (e.g., Rubinshtein, 1946). It should be noted, however, that Leontiev's interpretation of the relationship between mind and activity was somewhat different from the position advocated by Rubinshtein. Leontiev extends and develops the original scope of Rubinshtein's principle of "unity and inseparability of consciousness and activity," in three respects. First, Leontiev states that psychological studies should not focus only on the "psychological aspect or facet of activity" (as suggested by Rubinshtein), such as the relationship between activity and subjective experiences. Instead, he maintained that the relevance of activity to psychology is of a more general nature: activity is of fundamental importance to psychology because of its special function, "the function of placing the subject in the objective reality and transforming this reality into a form of subjectivity" (Leontiev, 1975, our translation). Second, as discussed below, Leontiev's analysis focuses on both conscious and unconscious mental phenomena. Third and finally, Leontiev offered a number of more concrete insights about the relationship between mind and activity, most notably the idea of structural similarity between internal and external processes.

THE CONCEPT OF ACTIVITY AND THE EVOLUTION OF PSYCHE

Leontiev started his professional career by taking part in a large-scale research program initiated and coordinated by Vygotsky. Later on he formulated his own agenda which was an ambitious attempt to provide a theoretical account of the evolution of mind.

The general idea of the mind being a special kind of organ emerging in evolution to help organisms survive has been part of Russian psychology since the 1920s. However, the idea remained an abstract statement, a philosophical claim rather than a theory. Leontiev's ambition was to translate this general statement into a concrete description of how the first phenomena that can be called "psyche" emerged in history, and how they developed into the current variety of mental phenomena. To accomplish this goal Leontiev needed a special kind of analytical tool, a concept more general than psyche, that would make it possible to define the context in which the psyche emerges and develops. An obvious candidate for such a concept is "life," since ultimately this is what undergoes evolutionary changes. However, this concept is too general and too vague. Instead, Leontiev chose "activity" as a concept that can provide a more concrete insight into what "life" is.

For Leontiev the phenomenon under consideration, the developing system he analyzed, was the mind, or psyche. Accordingly, the first challenge was to find the earliest, most elementary form of psyche as it emerged in evolution. The task was anything but trivial. There were a number of views regarding when exactly in biological evolution psyche appears for the first time. Is psyche a property of all living organisms? Must the "evolutionary threshold" be raised to include only animals having central nervous system? Only humans? Since answers to these questions were, quite understandably, based on logical arguments and beliefs rather than empirical evidence, it was hardly possible to establish with certainty which of the answers, if any, was correct. Therefore, the problem remained open and a space was left for suggesting new possible solutions. Leontiev did just that by developing his own line of arguments and proposing his own hypothesis about the emergence of psyche in biological evolution. These arguments and hypothesis can be summarized as follows.

A characteristic feature of all biological organisms is their ability to actively respond to environmental factors, that is, their "responsiveness." Organisms are not passively influenced by the environment; they develop their own internal and external responses using their own energy. This responsiveness, according to Leontiev, can be of two different types. First, organisms can respond to stimuli that produce direct biological effects. For instance, food may trigger digestive processes and can be actively assimilated by an organism, while changes in the ambient temperature may result in responses directed at maintaining an organism's own temperature within certain limits. Another type of responsiveness takes place when an organism responds to a stimulus that does not produce a direct biological effect. A smell of food or a sound signifying danger can elicit a strong response without immediately affecting the organism's biology. This second type of responsiveness, called "sensitivity," that is, an ability to respond to signals carrying biologically significant information, was considered by Leontiev the most basic manifestation of psyche.

Since the inception of sensitivity there have been two main lines of development of organisms in biological evolution. The first line is the development of the ability to maintain basic life support processes such as digestion. The second line is development of the ability to interact with the environment which results in the acquisition of new perceptual, cognitive, and motor functions and organs, such as senses, a nervous system, and limbs.

Having identified the most basic form of psyche, Leontiev went on to trace the development of progressively more advanced forms of psyche caused by dialectical contradictions between organisms and their environments. Changes in the environment, on the one hand, and acquisition of more sophisticated forms of interaction with the environment, on the other hand, were considered a driving force behind the development.

The emergence of psyche itself was, according to Leontiev, caused by a radical change in the life conditions of biological organisms: a transition from living in a homogeneous "primordial soup," in which life originally appeared, to living in an environment consisting of discrete things, or objects. Objects are characterized by relatively stable combinations of properties. Some of these properties, which are of direct biological importance, are systematically associated with other properties, which are not. The latter, therefore, can be used as signals indicating the former. As a result, organisms that develop sensitivity, an ability to respond to signals, have better chances of survival in an environment composed of distinct objects, compared to organisms that do not have such ability.

Leontiev discerned three stages of the development of psychological functions in animals: the sensory stage, the perceptual stage, and the intelligence stage. At the sensory stage, organisms recognize and respond to isolated attributes of the environment. Most animals are at a more advanced, perceptual stage of development, at which they can recognize whole objects and their relations. For instance, when they see that an obstacle between them and a food is removed, they go to the food directly. Some animals, such as apes, reach the highest stage in Leontiev's hierarchy of animal psyche, the intelligence stage. These animals are able to develop sophisticated mental representations of problem situations in which they are immediately engaged.

The concept of activity plays a crucial role in Leontiev's analysis of the evolution of psyche. The concept was introduced as fundamental as soon as Leontiev set out to discover the earliest manifestations of mind:

I will call the processes of activity the specific processes through which a live, that is, active relation of the subject to reality is realized, as opposed to other types of processes (Leontiev, 1981).

Immediately after introducing the concept of activity Leontiev introduced the concept of the object of activity. He emphasized that activities cannot exist without their objects: "Any activity of an organism is directed at a certain object; an 'objectless' activity is impossible" (Leontiev, 1981).

A distinction between mental and non-mental phenomena required that both be defined in terms of a general overarching concept and then differentiated within this frame of reference. Activity was chosen by Leontiev to play the role of such a basic, fundamental concept. He used this concept to describe the transition to more advanced forms of life associated with mental phenomena, as

. . . a transition from a "pre-mental" activity, that is, activity, which is not mediated by a representation of objective reality, to activity, which is mediated by a representation of objective reality. . . . Therefore, psyche, mental activity, is not something that is added to life but a special form of life, inevitably emerging in the process of its development (Leontiev, 1981).

Therefore, two historical threads can be discerned in Leontiev's analysis of the evolution of psyche. The first thread is a long-term project dealing with developmental transformations of the mind. The second thread is a development of the key analytical tool used by Leontiev in his historical analysis, the concept of activity. The meaning of the concept was substantially elaborated upon when Leontiev went on to discuss the development of the *human* mind, a radically new phase in the evolution of the psyche.

For animals, mind is an organ of survival; it increases the organism's fitness regarding its natural environment, just as claws or fur do. Through assuring the survival of the fittest, evolution stimulates the development of mind in animals. However, with the emergence of human culture and society, biological evolution ceased to be the main factor in the development of the mind. The survival of an individual living in society depends on economics, politics, and technologies, rather than fitness understood as the ability to adapt the body to the natural environment. Accordingly, the nature of the human mind is determined not only by biological factors but also by culture and society.

Leontiev specifically analyzed three aspects of culture that have a fundamental impact on the mind: tools, language, and the division of labor.

In his analysis of the role of tools and language, Leontiev by and large followed the approach established by Vygotsky. Tools were considered a vehicle for transmitting human experience from generation to generation. The structure of a tool itself, as well as learning how to use a tool, change the structure of human interaction with the world. By appropriating a tool, and integrating it into activities, human beings also appropriate the experience accumulated in the culture. Elaborate practices revolving around creating, organizing, and maintaining tools are vital accomplishments of human beings, differentiating us from other animals.

The use of tools is closely related to other factors influencing the development of the mind, namely, the use of language and the division of labor. Continuing the cultural-historical tradition of using the tool metaphor for understanding the role of signs and symbols in the functioning and development of the mind, Leontiev focused on the role of tools in the development of concepts. Concepts have a general meaning applicable to a variety of concrete situations and experiences. Over the course of their individual development (ontogenesis), human beings learn and appropriate concepts already existing in their cultures. The concepts, however, have not always been there. They are a result of the positive and negative experiences of people who contributed to the development of the culture. One might ask: How did the first concepts, first generalizations emerge from individual human experience? Leontiev suggested a hypothesis that may provide an answer, at least a partial one, to this question.

Early tools, such as a stone axe, could be used for a variety of purposes. They could, for example, cut trees, kill animals, or dig soil. The objects to which an axe was applied could be soft or hard. Some objects were easy to cut, some required substantial time and effort, and some were so hard that it was impossible even to leave a dent on them. Despite these differences, all the objects could be compared against the axe, which was an invariant component of all encounters. Therefore, the axe could be considered an embodied standard of softness/hardness. Using the axe for practical purposes to do something with an object in the environment had the side effect of placing the object on a "scale" of softness/hardness. This scale emerged as a generalization of the individual experience of using the tool. Since people followed shared, culturally developed procedures of creating and using tools, the tools could serve as an embodiment of abstract concepts based on the generalization of both individual and collective experience.

Another implication of the use of tools for historical development of the human mind is their role in the emergence of the division of labor. Even though the division of labor was the result of a variety of factors, it was tools that assured the development of the sophisticated forms of coordination typical of collaborative work and other socially distributed activities. On the one hand, the production of tools became a separate activity that required specialized skills. Individuals who possessed these skills were likely to make tools for other members of a social group, which was probably one of the first examples of the division of labor. On the other hand, tools and other artifacts (such as clothes) could facilitate coordination of individual contributions to collective activities by signifying the social status and specific responsibilities of their owners.

The division of labor, according to Leontiev, had a special significance for the development of the mind. When a person participates in a socially distributed work activity, his actions are typically motivated by one object but directed to another one. Let us consider Leontiev's canonical example of activity, a collective activity of primordial hunting. Individuals participating in a collective hunt may be divided into two groups: one group scares the animals and makes them move in a certain direction by beating the bushes (the beaters), and another group hides waiting to ambush the animals directed towards them by the beaters (the ambushers). Both groups are motivated by food. However, for beaters, the immediate goal is not to get closer to the animals and kill them but, on the contrary, to scare them away. These hunters are motivated by their share of the whole catch which they expect to receive as a reward for their contribution to the hunt. Taken out of the context of collective activity, the actions of the beaters appear to have no meaning.

A non-coincidence of objects that motivate an activity and objects at which the activity is directed is a characteristic feature of human activity. In animal activities, motivating objects and directing objects basically coincide. If the activity of an animal is directed towards an object, this object typically immediately corresponds to a certain need. In human activities, however, the link between what an individual is doing and what they are trying to attain through what they are doing is often difficult to establish. The structure of human activities, as opposed to the structure of the activities of other animals, can be extremely complex. The main reason behind this, according to Leontiev, is a transformation individual activities undergo as a result of participation in the division of labor. When an individual takes part in a socially distributed activity, the difference between motivating and directing objects is forced upon the individual by the organization of the socially distributed activity. The division of labor makes dissociation between motivation and direction of activity an objective attribute of an individual's interaction with the world. Internalization of this dissociation changes the structure of individual activities. Individual activities can potentially develop a complex relationship between motivating and directing objects.

In a way, the historical evolution of mind illustrates the "universal law of psychological development" formulated by Vygotsky for individual development: new functions and attributes first emerge as distributed between the individual and their social environment (that is, as inter-psychological ones) and then become appropriated by individuals (that is, become intra-psychological ones). The division of labor makes attaining a goal within a collective activity meaningful (or at least rewarded) even if the relation of the goal to the object of the activity as a whole is not straightforward. The ability to connect the current focus of one's efforts with their ultimate intended outcome and to integrate indirectly related actions first emerges in history as supported by the division of labor. At this stage of development, the ability to coordinate intermediate goals can only exist as distributed between people. For instance, the beaters in the hunt above could perform their roles without understanding the actual meaning of the actions. Arguably, however, collective activities can be carried out much more successfully if contributing individuals understand the relationship between intermediate and ultimate outcomes. Therefore, the division of labor creates conditions for dissociation between motives and goals. This dissociation first emerges in collective activities and then in individual activities and minds.

THE STRUCTURE OF HUMAN ACTIVITY
NEEDS, MOTIVES, AND THE OBJECT OF ACTIVITY

So far we have discussed "activity" in a broad sense, as subject-object interaction in general. In this broad meaning, any process of a subject's interaction with the world can be qualified as an activity. However, in activity theory, the term activity also has another, narrower meaning. According to this meaning, activity refers to a specific level of subject-object interaction, the level at which the object has the status of a motive. A motive is an object that meets a certain need of the subject. The reason the notion of motive plays a key role in the conceptual framework of activity theory will be evident from the discussion below.

Let us consider more closely the idea of subject-object interaction taking place at several levels simultaneously. Obviously, a whole range of objects with which a subject is interacting can be discerned at any given moment. For instance, depending on the angle from which a person is viewed, they can be described as hitting a key on a computer keyboard, typing a word, or writing a novel. Accordingly, the objects the person is dealing with include the key, the word, and the novel, all at the same time. These objects constitute a hierarchy, where objects located higher in the hierarchy define larger-scale units of subject-object interaction. The top-level object in the hierarchy, according to activity theory, has a special status. The reason the subject is attempting to attain this object is the object itself. The object is perceived as something that can meet a need of the subject. In other words, the object motivates the subject, it is a motive.

Activity in a narrow sense is a unit of subject-object interaction defined by the motive. It is a system of processes oriented towards the motive where the meaning of any individual component of the system is determined by its role in attaining the motive.

Therefore, according to activity theory, the ultimate cause behind human activities is needs. Needs can be viewed, according to Leontiev, from either a biological perspective or psychological perspective. From a biological perspective a need is an objective requirement of an organism. Having a need means that something should be available in the environment to satisfy the requirement. Organisms may need food, water, air, or temperature maintained in an appropriate range, in order to survive and reproduce. From a psychological perspective, a need is a directedness of activities towards the world, towards bringing about desirable changes in the environment. It is expressed in particular behavior and subjective experiences.

At the psychological level, needs can be represented in two different ways. Needs which are not "objectified," that is, not associated with a concrete object cause general excitement which stimulates the search for an object to satisfy the need. The subject may experience discomfort ("a need state"). However, this discomfort cannot direct the subject and help satisfy the need, except in stimulating an exploratory behavior that is not directed at anything in particular. When a need meets its object, which, according to Leontiev, is "a moment of extraordinary importance" (Leontiev, 1978), the need itself is transformed, that is, objectified. When a need becomes coupled with an object, an activity emerges. From that moment on, the object becomes a motive and the need not only stimulates but also directs the subject. An unobjectified need can be defined as a raw state of need looking for an object, while an objectified need means that the subject knows what it is looking for.

Therefore, the most fundamental property of needs, according to Leontiev, is that they cannot be separated from objects. The defining feature of unobjectified needs is that they are seeking for objects, while objectified needs manifest themselves through their objects. The very concept of activity includes its orientation towards an object, an object that both motivates and directs the activity. The object of activity, which is defined by Leontiev as the "true motive" of an activity (Leontiev, 1978), is the most important attribute differentiating one activity from another.

Human needs are different from other animals' needs. Psychological needs of other animals are related to biological needs, and their activities are directed towards objects associated with biological needs. However, even in non-human animals, biological needs do not directly determine the objects of the needs. When selecting objects of their activities, animals can rely on a wide range of attributes which are only indirectly related to biological properties. This ability provides obvious advantages. For instance, a lion that attacks slower antelopes might survive longer than a lion that attacks indiscriminately. The more developed an animal, the more its psychological needs are influenced by the structure and affordances of the environment, and the more difficult it is to trace the behavior of the animal to underlying biological needs.

In humans, some psychological needs are clearly based on biological needs. However, even these needs are transformed by culture and society which provide incentives, guidance, and constraints on selecting the objects of the needs and the means of satisfying the needs. More importantly, human psychological needs are not limited to needs based on biology. The relationship of human psychological needs to biology is difficult or impossible to trace, and sometimes this relationship appears to be negative rather than positive. Some cultural practices and many rituals do not seem to be healthy, sensible, or even pleasant.

Activity theory neither proposes a taxonomy of potentially effective needs (as do some psychological approaches, e.g., Maslow (1968)) nor does it provide strict criteria to differentiate motives from non-motives. Human needs are always developing, so it is impossible in principle to give a definitive description of all possible needs and motives. What activity theory does propose is a conceptual framework to bridge the gap between motivation and action. Activity theory provides a coherent account for processes at various levels of acting in the world.

ACTIVITIES, ACTIONS, AND OPERATIONS

Activities are not monolithic. Each activity can be represented as a hierarchical structure organized into three layers. The top layer is the activity itself, which is oriented towards a motive. The motive is the object, which stimulates, excites the subject. It is the object that the subject ultimately needs to attain.

However, human activities are typically not directed straight towards their motives. As in the hunters example above, socially distributed activities are characterized by dissociation between motivating and directing objects. Complex relations between these two types of objects are present in society and are a fact of life for people who live in the society. Participation in social activities makes it necessary for individual subjects to differentiate between (a) objects that attract them and (b) objects at which their activities are directed.

In other words, an activity is composed of a sequence of steps, each of which may not be immediately related to the motive. According to activity theory terminology, these steps are *actions*. The objects at which they are directed are called goals. Goals are conscious; human beings are typically aware of the goals they want to attain. In contrast, we may not be immediately aware of motives. Leontiev observed that making motives conscious requires a special effort of making sense of "indirect evidence," i.e., ". . . motives are revealed to consciousness only objectively by means of analysis of activity and its dynamics. Subjectively, they appear only in their oblique expression, in the form of experiencing wishes, desires, or striving toward a goal" (Leontiev, 1978).

Actions, in their turn, can also be decomposed into lower-level units of activity, operations. Operations are routine processes providing an adjustment of an action to the ongoing situation. They are oriented towards the conditions under which the subject is attaining a goal. People are typically not aware of operations. Operations may emerge as an "improvisation," as a result of a spontaneous adjustment of an action on the fly. For example, when walking in a crowd, one can carry out elaborate maneuvering to avoid colliding with other people and physical obstacles without even realizing it. Another source of new operations is automatization of actions. Over the course of learning and frequent execution, a conscious action may transform into a routine operation. For instance, some skills, which in experienced car drivers are apparently operations, result from many hours of practice. When first learning to drive a car, a novice may need to consciously focus on the procedure of, for example, changing lanes. Changing lanes for inexperienced drivers can be an action that requires total concentration and makes it impossible to be engaged in any other activity (such as conversation). However, gradually this action may become more and more automatic. Eventually a driver reaches the phase at which changing lanes is done automatically and is hardly noticed. The driver can now also engage in other simultaneous activities.

The separation between actions and operations according to their orientation—respectively, towards the goal and towards the conditions in which the goal is "given" to the subject—is relative rather than absolute. Some actions are more directly related to the object of activity than others. For instance, adding a new section to a draft document is clearly related to the goal of writing a paper. However, accomplishing this goal may require a range of auxiliary actions, more loosely related to the goal at hand. One may need to respond to other people's comments, learn new features of a word processor, such as styles or "Track changes," or find information in physical or electronic archives. Therefore, the main criterion separating actions from operations is that operations are automatized.

Levels of activity, shown in Figure 2.2, can transform into one another. Automatization is an example of transformations between actions and operations. Over the course of practice actions can become automatic operations. The opposite process is "de-automatization," the transformation of routine operations to conscious actions. Such a transformation can take place, for instance, when an automatized operation fails to produce the desired outcome and the individual reflects on the reasons for the failure and on how the operation can be "fixed." Typically, a new, more appropriate procedure is devised which first is carried out as a conscious action and then becomes an operation. Transformations can also take place between activities and actions. For instance, a goal subordinated to another, higher-level goal can become a motive, so that a former action acquires the status of an activity.

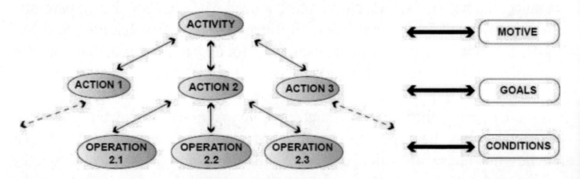

Figure 2.2: The hierarchical structure of activity. Activities are composed of actions, which are, in turn, composed of operations (left). These three levels correspond, respectively, to the motive, goals, and conditions, as indicated by bi-directional arrows.

FUNCTIONAL ORGANS

An activity-theoretical concept of special relevance to HCI is the concept of functional organs. The origins of this concept can be traced back to earlier works, for instance, those by the Russian physiologist Ukhtomsky, who defined functional organ in a broad sense as: "Any temporary combination of forces which is capable of attaining a definite end" (Ukhtomsky, 1978, cited in Zinchenko, 1996). Leontiev (1981) elaborated this concept by introducing the idea of functional organs as created by individuals through the combination of both internal and external resources. Functional organs combine natural human capabilities with artifacts to allow the individual to attain goals that could not be attained otherwise. For instance, human eyes in combination with eyeglasses, binoculars, microscopes, or night vision devices, constitute functional organs of vision that may significantly extend human abilities.

To create and use functional organs, individuals need special kinds of competencies (Kaptelinin, 1996b). Tool-related competencies include knowledge about the functionality of a tool, as well as skills necessary to operate it. Task-related competencies include knowledge about the higher-level goals attainable with the use of a tool, and skills of translating these goals into the tool's functionality.

One implication of the notion of functional organs is that distribution of activities between the mind and artifacts is always functional. It only takes place within subsystems that have specific functions, more or less clearly defined. Such subsystems, whether distributed or not, are integral parts of the subject, who makes ultimate decisions on when to use functional organs and whether they have to be updated, modified, or even completely abandoned. Therefore, the subject must have competencies of a special type to create and use functional organs efficiently. These competencies, which can be labeled as meta-functional, provide integration of functional organs into the system of human activities as a whole (Kaptelinin, 1996b). In contrast to tool-related competencies and task-related competencies, meta-functional competencies are not directly related to employing functional organs for reaching goals. Instead, they deal with the coordination of multiple goals that can be attained via one action, with limitations of functional organs (for instance, which goals cannot be achieved with them), and with side effects, maintenance, and troubleshooting.

BASIC PRINCIPLES OF LEONTIEV'S ACTIVITY THEORY: AN OVERVIEW

The main ideas and assumptions of activity theory, outlined above, have been elaborated by Leontiev into a set of more specific notions, claims, and arguments. Kaptelinin and Nardi (2006), building on Wertsch (1981), identify the following principles:

Object-orientedness. The principle of object-orientedness states that all human activities are directed toward their objects and are differentiated from one another by their respective objects. Objects motivate and direct activities, around them activities are coordinated, and in them activities are crystallized when the activities are complete. Analysis of objects is therefore a necessary requirement for understanding human activities, both individual and collective ones. This principle (which bears some similarity to phenomenology's notion of "intentionality;" see Dourish, 2001) is directly related to the very concept of activity as a "subject-object" relationship. A subject's interaction with the world is structured; it is organized around objects[5]. Objects have their "objective" meanings, determined by their relationship with other entities existing in the world (including the subject himself or herself). In order to meet their needs, the subject has to reveal the objective meaning of the objects and act accordingly.

The principle of object-orientedness applies differently to animals and human beings. Animals live in a structured world of natural objects which are material and mostly have direct positive or negative meanings and values, provide affordances for action, and so forth. Human beings live in a predominantly man-made world, where objects are not necessarily physical things: they can be intangible, but they can still be considered "objects" as long as they objectively exist in the world. For instance, the objects of learning a new language or making a company profitable are impossible to touch, physically weigh, or measure with a ruler. However, the grammatical structure of a language or profit margin of a company does not exist merely in a person's imagination. Rather, they are "facts of life," which need to be faced and dealt with. "Objective" is understood in activity theory in a broad sense as including not only the properties of things that can be directly registered with physical instruments, but also socially and culturally defined properties.

Hierarchical structure of activity. Human activities, according to Leontiev, are units of life which are organized into three hierarchical layers (see Figure 2.2). The top layer is the activity itself, which is oriented toward a motive, corresponding to a certain need. The motive is the object that the subject ultimately needs to attain.

For instance, in some cultural contexts people reaching a certain age need to learn how to drive a car (and get a driver's license); it is a general prerequisite of being a fully functional member of society. Learning how to drive a car is an activity organized as a multilayer system of sub-units directed at getting a driver's license.

Actions are conscious processes directed at goals which must be undertaken to fulfill the object. Goals can be decomposed into sub-goals, sub-sub-goals, and so forth. For instance, one may decide to enroll in a driving school, purchase instructional materials, make a schedule of theoretical lessons and practice sessions.

Actions are implemented through lower-level units of activity called operations. Operations are routine processes providing an adjustment of an action to the ongoing situation. They are oriented toward the conditions under which the subject is trying to attain a goal. People are typically not aware of their operations. For instance, a driving school student taking notes during a lecture might be fully concentrated on traffic rules rather than the process of writing. Operations emerge in two ways. First, an operation can be a result of step-by-step automatization of an originally conscious action (e.g., over time, the action of changing lanes may transform into a routine operation that does not require any conscious control). When such operations fail, they are often transformed into conscious actions again. Second, an operation can be a result of "improvisation," a spontaneous adjustment of an action on the fly, e.g., in an emergency situation the driver may act "instinctively," without thinking.

The three-layer model only applies to human activities. Complex relationships between motives (i.e., what motivates the activity) and goals (i.e., what directs the activity) are a characteristic feature of humans. While animals usually act directly toward the objects that motivate them (e.g., food), humans often attain their motives by directing their efforts to other things. For example, however hungry they might be, diners usually grab a menu rather than the first available food upon entering a restaurant.

Considering human activity as a three-layer system opens up a possibility for a combined analysis of motivational, goal-directed, and operational aspects of human acting in the world, that is, bringing together the issues of Why, What, and How within a consistent conceptual framework (Bødker, 1991).

Realizing this possibility in a concrete study may, however, be problematic. Revealing the ultimate motives of a person or the fine-grain structure of automatic operations may prove to be difficult, if not impossible. This limitation of Leontiev's three-layer model as an analytical tool can be overcome by employing an expansive "actions first" strategy. This strategy involves starting analysis from the actions layer which relatively easily yields itself to qualitative research methods. In particular, people are usually aware of their goals and can report or express them in a certain way. Then the analysis can be expanded both "up," to progressively higher level goals and, ultimately, motives, and "down," to sub-goals and operations. The expanding scope of analysis may not cover the entire structure of the activity in question but be sufficient for the purposes of the task at hand (see also Kaptelinin et al., 1999).

Mediation. Arguably, mediation is the primary dimension along which human beings differ from other animals. It is mediation that has made homo sapiens such a successful species. While we do not have sharp claws and thick fur, we compensate by employing mediating artifacts such as hammers, knives, and warm clothes. In fact, all key distinctive features of humans, such as language, society, and culture, the production and use of advanced tools, all involve mediation. They represent different aspects of the same phenomenon, that is, the emergence of a complex system of objects and structures, both material and immaterial, which serve as mediating means embedded in the interaction between human beings and the world.

Activity theory inherits its special interest in mediation from the approach that made the most fundamental impact on Leontiev's framework —that is, Vygotsky's cultural-historical psychology. Vygotsky's ideas concerning mediation were explicitly incorporated into the conceptual framework of activity theory but placed in a somewhat different theoretical context. Since the overall focus of Leontiev's approach was on activity, understood as the purposeful interaction of active subjects with the objective world, rather than particular higher mental functions and their ontogenetic development, activity theory is specifically concerned with tools as means that mediate activity as a whole, rather than signs, that is, means that mediate specific mental operations.

Tool mediation allows for appropriating socially developed forms of acting in the world. Tools reflect the previous experience of other people accumulated in the structural properties of tools, such as their shape or material, as well as in the knowledge of how the tool should be used (see Figure 2.3). Therefore, the use of tools is a form of accumulation and transmission of social, cultural knowledge. Tools not only shape the external behavior; as discussed below, through internalization, they also influence the mental functioning of individuals. For instance, a person's cognitive map of a city may depend on whether or not the person is a car driver. A software developer understands the abstraction of layers of a software architecture. This understanding is actionable, and he or she does not need to be looking at a diagram of an architecture to use the knowledge in a design task.

Internalization and externalization. This principle states that human activities are distributed—and dynamically re-distributed—along the external/internal dimension. Any human activity contains both internal and external components. Sometimes external components are hardly visible: they can be reduced, for instance, to eye movements or even patterns of brain activation, but they are always present. The concepts of internalization and externalization refer to the processes of mutual transformations between internal and external components of an activity.

In the process of internalization, external components become internal. For instance, young children often use their fingers for simple arithmetic, but over time the use of fingers typically becomes redundant. An inexperienced driver may speak aloud to remind himself of the "parallel parking" procedure, but the need for speaking aloud disappears with practice.

The process, opposite to internalization, is externalization—that is, transformation of internal components of an activity into external ones. An example of externalization is sketching a design idea.

Externalization is the basis of all human culture. It is a uniquely human capacity. Tools motivate and enable externalization. The very existence of a pencil incurs momentum for an artist to externalize something she imagines. Tools excite and propel us. The capacities of a tool afford what is entirely remarkable—a person's thoughts, ideas, dreams, reasoning, change to materially visible form. The artist herself reacts to what she draws, perhaps altering it once she sees how it looks. She may choose to share the drawing with others or abandon it. Tools thrill us, and they therefore entail morality because they will cause us to act. The tools we imagine and construct alter us and the world through externalization.

In a similar vein, an activity which is initially socially distributed that is, distributed between several people can be appropriated by a person (i.e., the learner) and then carried out individually. The opposite process is the transformation of an individual activity into a socially distributed one, e.g., when a person initiates a group project or other people intervene to help an individual to carry out her actions (Cole and Engeström, 1993). The dimensions of internal/external and individual/social are similar to one another in many respects and are closely related. For instance, when an internal activity is externalized, it also affects the individual-collective dimension: for instance, tools and signs employed in externally distributed actions can be shared and thus enable social distribution of the actions.

Development. Finally, activity theory requires that activities always be analyzed in the context of development. Development in activity theory is both an object of study and research strategy. As an object of study, development constitutes a complex phenomenon that can be analyzed at different levels. Examples of the levels of analysis include studying the development of various forms of animal activity in biological evolution (phylogenesis), emergence of specifically human forms of activity in social history (sociogenesis), individual development throughout various phases of life (ontogenesis), and appropriation of particular artifacts (instrumental genesis, Rabardel and Bourmaud, 2003).

As a research strategy, development requires that any object of study should be analyzed in the dynamics of its transformation over time[6]. Accordingly, activity theory prioritizes formative experiments over traditional controlled experiments. Formative experiments combine active intervention in the system or processes under study with monitoring of developmental changes caused by the intervention. At the same time, activity theory does not prescribe a single method of study since different types and levels of development require different methods or combinations of methods.

The principles of activity theory, described above, comprise an integrated system: they represent different aspects of human activity as a whole. Systematic application of any of the principles makes it necessary to eventually engage some (or even all) of the others. For instance, analysis of the effects of certain technologies on human cognition from an activity theoretical perspective would require identifying the variety of activities, as well as their respective objects within which the technologies are being employed (object-orientedness), the role and place of the technologies in the hierarchical structure of each of these activities (hierarchical structure), how the activities are being re-shaped by using the technologies as mediating means (mediation), and how transformations of external components of activity are related to corresponding changes of internal components (internalization and internalization). And all these phenomena should be analyzed as they unfold over time (development).

ENGESTRÖM'S ACTIVITY SYSTEM MODEL

Leontiev's approach is predominantly concerned with activities of individual human beings. While Leontiev explicitly mentions that activities can be carried out not only by individuals but by social entities (collective subjects), too, he does not systematically explore the structure and development of collective activities and does not present a conceptual model of collective activity (which can probably be explained, at least partly, by the ideology-related limitations and constraints that were imposed on studies of social phenomena in the USSR). A model of collective activity, the "activity system model" (a.k.a. "Engeström's triangle") was proposed by the Finnish educational researcher Yrjö Engeström (1987). The model is a result of a two-step extension of Leontiev's original concept of activity—that is, activity understood as "subject-object" interaction—to the case of collective activity.

The first step, the most significant revision of Leontiev's notion of activity as subject-object interaction, was adding a third element, "community," which resulted in a structure comprising a three-way interaction between "subject," "object," and "community." This structure can be represented as a down-pointing triangle (see Figure 2.3). Second, it was suggested that each of the three particular interactions within the structure is mediated by a special type of means. Concrete mediational means for these interactions, according to Engeström, are: (a) tools/instruments for the subject-object interaction (as also posited by Leontiev), (b) rules for the subject-community interaction, and (c) division of labor for the community-object interaction. In addition, the model includes the outcome of the activity system as a whole: a transformation of the object produced by the activity in question into an intended result, which can be utilized by other activity systems. The complete model is shown in Figure 2.4.

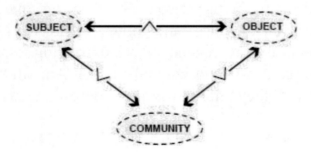

Figure 2.3: Three-way (mediated) interaction between subject, object, and community (adapted from Engeström, 1987).

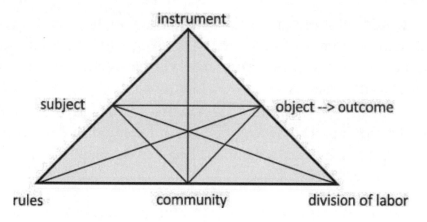

Figure 2.4: Engeström's activity system model.

As an example, consider the activity of an interaction designer who works as a member of a design team redesigning the user interface of a computer application. The object of the activity is the existing interface, and the expected outcome is a new interface. The interaction designer employs a variety of tools in her work on the object, including physical objects (e.g., computers), software (e.g., development environments), and methods and techniques (e.g., personas). The community comprises other members of the team such as interaction designers, the project manager, and technicians. The interaction designer's relation with the community is mediated by explicit and implicit rules, e.g., taking part in project meetings, and receiving certain financial rewards. Furthermore, producing the outcome of the activity system as a whole, a new interface, is the responsibility of the entire design team: the effort of the interaction designer is a part of a larger effort of the team. Therefore, the work of the interaction designer needs to be coordinated with the work of other team members. This coordination is achieved by employing a division of labor, which mediates the relation between the design team and its object.

When studying complex real-life phenomena, applying one activity system model is often not sufficient. Such phenomena need to be represented as networks of activity systems. For instance, redesigning the user interface of a computer application can be a part of an even larger-scale effort, involving several design teams, directed at developing a new version of the computer application in question. Redesigning the user interface in that case would provide a partial outcome which would need to be integrated with outcomes of other activity systems (e.g., a team developing new functionality of the product) to achieve the overarching purpose of a network of activity systems.

A key tenet of Engeström's framework is that activity systems are constantly developing. The development is understood in a dialectical sense as a process driven by contradictions. Engeström identifies four types of contradictions in activity systems:

1. First-level contradictions are inner contradictions of each of the components of an activity system: subject, object, community, instruments, rules, and division of labor. For instance, the mediating means used by a physician include various medications which, on the one hand, have certain medical effects, and, on the other hand, are products with associated costs, legal regulations, and distribution channels. This double nature of medications may affect the specific decisions made by the physician. For instance, the cost of the best possible medication may be prohibitive, which may make a physician choose a more affordable alternative.

2. Second-level contradictions are those that arise between the components of an activity system. For instance, a certain type of medical treatment may be unsuitable for certain patients.

3. Third-level contradictions describe potential problems emerging in the relationship between the existing forms of an activity system and its potential, more advanced object and outcome. The advancement of an activity system as a whole may be undermined by the resistance to change, demonstrated by the existing organization of the activity system.

4. Finally, fourth-level contradictions refer to contradictions within a network of activity systems, that is, between an activity system and other activity systems involved in the production of a joint outcome. For instance a positive effect of surgery (i.e., a partial outcome produced by the activity system of a surgical department of a hospital), can be undermined by an improper follow-up rehabilitation (i.e., a

partial outcome produced by the activity system of another organization, such as an outpatient physical therapy clinic).

The activity system model has been employed in a range of disciplines, especially education and organizational learning (see, e.g., CRADLE, Center for Research on Activity, Development and Learning, n.d.). See Spinuzzi (2011) for a critique of Engeström's evolving notions of the concept of object.

CURRENT DIVERSITY OF ACTIVITY THEORETICAL FRAMEWORKS

The approaches developed by, respectively, Leontiev and Engeström are currently the most common variants of activity theory. The approaches provide complementary perspectives on human activities. Leontiev's variant mostly focuses on individuals understood as social creatures acting in social contexts. Engeström's activity system model, on the other hand, is predominantly concerned with collective activities carried out by groups and organizations whose activities are implemented through contributions —i.e., actions—of individual subjects.

In addition, a number of other current frameworks are partly influenced by activity theory and partly built upon other approaches. Such frameworks include, for instance, instrumental genesis (Rabardel and Bourmaud, 2003), genre tracing (Spinuzzi, 2003), and the systemic-structural activity theory (Bedny and Harris, 2005).

---

[2]Leontiev himself usually referred to his framework as "activity approach" ("dejatelnostnyj podhod"), or "activity approach in psychology," rather than "activity theory" (cf. Mescherjakov and Zinchenko, 2003).

[3]This warning, in our view, should be extended to the widespread use of the distinction between technical and psychological tools, assigned to Vygotsky, in current research. This useful conceptual distinction is difficult to practically apply to concrete, real-life cases. The same object can be a technical or a psychological tool depending on the way it is used. For instance, a knife is a technical tool when it is used to slice a sausage but it is a psychological tool when it is used by a robber to frighten his victim into submission. Therefore, the border between technical and psychological tools is

not clear-cut. They should rather be considered two different aspects of the same artifact, often intertwined in a complex way. For instance, a pen is a technical tool in the sense that it is used to change a thing (e.g., to write a note on a piece of paper) but at the same time it is a psychological tool, since it is used to write a message intended to affect people.

[4]Internalization was the object of study in an empirical investigation conducted by Leontiev under Vygotsky's supervision (Leontiev, 1981). The study employed a method called "double stimulation," created by Vygotsky specifically for studies of the development of higher psychological functions. The main feature of this method is presenting the subject with two sets of stimuli. The first, primary set is comprised of stimuli used by the subject to solve an experimental task. The task could be—as it was in Leontiev's study—remembering a set of words (stimuli) for subsequent recall. The subjects are also provided with another, secondary set of stimuli as auxiliary means for performing the task. Stimuli of the secondary set are signs referring to the stimuli of the primary set. The aim of using the method of double stimulation was to compare problem solving with and without secondary sets of stimuli. The design allowed for the analysis of the impact of mediation on subjects' performance in various cognitive tasks.

In the study conducted by Leontiev, the double stimulation method was employed as follows. Subjects of three age groups—pre-school children, middle school children, and university students—were presented with lists of words with the instruction to remember the words. After the presentation the subjects were asked to recall as many words as possible. The lists of words constituted primary sets of stimuli. Each group of subjects was divided into two sub-groups corresponding to two experimental conditions. In one condition the words were the only stimuli presented. In another condition the subjects were given a secondary set of stimuli, a stack of picture cards, which they could use as mnemonic tools. For instance, to remember the word "dinner," a subject could select a picture of an onion and lay it away. Layaway cards could be used by the subjects during the recall phase of the experiment.

It was found that performance in each of these conditions improved with age and that using cards generally improved performance. However, the difference between recalling words with and without cards was manifested differently in the three age groups. In pre-school children, the performance was rather poor and approximately at the same level in both conditions. In middle school children the usage of cards resulted in a marked increase in performance level compared to the no-cards condition. University students showed a high level of performance in both conditions, and the difference between the conditions was small.

The data were interpreted by Leontiev as an indication that children of the three age groups were at different levels in the development of mediated memory. Pre-school children had not yet developed mediation capabilities, so they could not benefit from using the cards. That was why there was little difference between their performance in the two conditions. Middle school children could successfully use the cards as external mediational tools and that was the reason they could substantially benefit from using the cards. Finally, the university students, according to Leontiev, reached similar levels of performance in both conditions because their memory was mediated whether or not they used the cards. When they could use the cards, they relied on them as external mediators. When no external mediators were provided, they used internal mediators, which were almost as effective as external mediators.

Empirical data from this and other studies employing the double stimulation technique (Vygotsky, 1982) supported the view of a re-structuring of mental processes as a result of development in a cultural environment. The re-structuring follows the stages of (a) no mediation, (b) external mediation, and (c) internal mediation resulting from internalization.

[5]There is a linguistic problem that makes adequate translation of Leontiev's notion of "object" from Russian to English somewhat complicated. In Russian there are two words with similar but distinct meanings: objekt and predmet. Both refer to objectively existing entities, but the notion of predmet typically also implies a relevance of the entity in question to certain human purposes or interests. Similar linguistic distinctions can be found in German and some other languages. Leontiev deliberately referred to the object of activity as predmet rather than objekt. However, this distinction is usually lost in English translation since both words are translated as "object."

[6]The developmental research perspective adopted by activity theory is often associated with dialectical logic, a concept and framework introduced by the Russian philosopher Evald Ilyenkov (Ilyenkov, 2008, see Engeström et al., 1999). Dialectical logic is different from traditional formal logic in how it views contradictions and development. Traditional logic invariantly considers contradictions as indicators of problems that need to be addressed. Contradictions are to be eliminated in order to create a perfectly logical system (either an abstract one, such as a model or theory, or a more concrete one, such as the management structure of an organization). In addition, traditional logic is typically not concerned with development; perfectly logical systems do not need to be changed and may stay as they are indefinitely.

Dialectical logic starts from a different assumption. It is assumed that dialectical development—that is, development driven by contradictions—is a fundamental aspect of all imaginable objects of study and therefore should be taken into consideration in analysis. While some "superficial" contradictions can be eliminated in a relatively straightforward way, there are also other, deeper contradictions that cannot be simply resolved once and for all. Any solution intended to resolve such contradictions is temporary, for it gives rise to new contradictions.

An example of a contradiction of this type, well known to HCI researchers, is the contradiction between tasks and artifacts. The notion of "task-artifact cycle" (Carroll, 1991) implies that the ultimate balance between tasks and artifacts cannot be achieved. A new artifact changes the task for which it is developed which means that another artifact needs to be developed to support the new task, and so on and so forth.

Dialectical logic posits that analysis of the object of study which only deals with how the object exists at the present time is insufficient. Instead, analysis of the development trajectory of the object—preferably, starting from an initial undeveloped form (i.e., a "germ")—is claimed to be critically important for understanding how the object has come to be what it is, and what contradictions can be expected to drive its further development.

CHAPTER 3

Agency

The term "agency" is used in many different ways. We examine its place in activity theory and suggest some extensions to notions of agency. The nature of agency is an old and ongoing debate. It has been reintroduced into contemporary social theory by actor-network theory (Latour, 1993; Law and Callon, 1992; see Kaptelinin and Nardi, 2006). We will suggest that different kinds of entities can exhibit different kinds of agency depending on circumstances. In other words, agency is not a simple property of a subject or thing. It is an important concept for HCI and activity theory because of the principle of mediation. Entities mediate according to the kinds of agency they are capable of.

For Leontiev, the primary type of agency was the agency of individual human subjects. We define human agency as the ability and the need to act. The most basic meaning of the "ability to act" is the ability to produce an effect, following standard dictionary definitions. However, this meaning is too broad for our purposes. If "acting" is understood as just producing an effect, then the ability to "act" is a property of anything that exists, either physically or ideally; any object, process, or idea. A narrower definition of acting is producing an effect according to an intention. The "need to act" encompasses biological and cultural needs. It is important to note that we use this distinction exclusively to refer to the origins of needs. Of course, all human needs are social in the sense that the way they are manifested and experienced is determined by the individual's development in social context. The criteria of what an individual considers healthy, attractive, prestigious, and so forth, are determined by the immediate and general cultural environment. The meaning of objects as things that can potentially meet the needs of an individual is established socially. For instance, religious norms can prescribe that potentially edible things are not perceived as food.

However, humans are animals too, and, as any animals, must meet their biological needs. Throughout biological evolution, a driving force of development has been meeting the basic needs of organisms. By "biological needs" we understand the needs that ensure survival and reproduction. The invisible evolutionary background of human agency means that biological needs are deeply ingrained in the nature of human agency. On the other hand, the human adaptation of culture created a powerful new set of needs. Cultural needs have the potential to change rapidly and to proliferate in number far beyond basic biological needs.

Intentions are driven by biological needs to ensure survival and reproduction, and by cultural needs established socially. Humans themselves are the realization of cultural needs expressed in the intentions of others. We embody cultural needs as a result of our activity and the activity of others who act on us. The surgeon's hands, the attorney's mind, the athlete's body—such agencies are the result of object-oriented activity. Those who act on us to make us who we are include family, friends, peers, teachers, coaches, and co-workers, as well as the wider culture.

A TYPOLOGY OF AGENTS

To gain a more nuanced view of agency, we move beyond the usual binary schemes. As can be seen in Table 3.1, we avoid binaries such as human-machine agency (Rose et al., 2005) and human-material agency (Pickering, 1993). Too much is obscured in such schemes. We theorize different kinds of entities that can be agents, as well as the possibility of delegating agency. We consider several dimensions as a basis for categorizing agents more flexibly. We argue that under varying circumstances, different kinds of agents may exhibit similar agencies.

Table 3.1 first makes a distinction between agents that are living or non-living. In Chapter 2 we established that not any entity is a subject. A subject lives in the world and has needs. Non-living things do not have needs.

Next, the table distinguishes between human and non-human living beings according to the kinds of needs they have. Humans have basic and cultural needs. Other living beings have basic needs only. We distinguish two kinds of non-human living beings: those that are the product of cultural needs and those that are not. The category "non-human living beings (cultural)" includes organisms such as domestic animals, plants, fungi, live vaccines, clones, and genetically engineered plants and animals. In other words, there are organisms that have evolved outside human intention and those that have been cultivated, cultured, husbanded, bred, cloned, or genetically modified. The latter result from some human activity motivated by a cultural need.

The dimension "realize intentions of humans" denotes things (natural) and things (cultural). Things that result from a human intention produced in a cultural milieu are artifacts. A speed bump slows a driver because it is designed to do so. A fence keeps in the sheep, a vaccine deters disease, a field of pumpkins is harvested for jack-o-lanterns. By contrast, an ocean current moves sea life with an agency that has no intention. A volcano erupts and covers a town with ash, a comet explodes. Effects ensue without intention.

The final column in Table 3.1 is social entities. Social entities are comprised of entities from all the other columns. They produce effects, and they can be said to have cultural needs (if they are to survive and reproduce themselves, certain things have to happen), and they realize human intentions. But because they are a composite of the other four entities, they have perhaps changed to a different level of abstraction for which the dimensions of the table are insufficient. However, the notion of macro-actors in actor-network theory suggests that social entities have "interests" and can be seen as agents in their own right. In actor-network theory, large-scale entities—for example, the European Union, Silicon Valley, the space program, high-tech, organized crime—can be said to have interests.

The cells in the leftmost column of the table identify different kinds of agencies. Rows 3-5 identify dimensions of these agencies. Row 3 indicates that all agents can produce effects. Row 4 indicates that when producing effects, some agents realize biological needs. Row 5 indicates that when producing effects, some agents realize cultural needs. Row 6 indicates that an agent may realize the intentions of (other) humans. For example, the Mars probe realizes the intentions of the scientists who built it. A schoolchild learning to read realizes the intentions of parents and teachers (and her own intentions in most cases).

Agencies	Agents	Things (natural)	Things (cultural)	Non-human living beings (natural)	Non-human living beings (cultural)	Human beings	Social entities
	Examples	tsunamis, Northern lights, vernal pools, Martian rocks	speed bumps, sewing machines, teapots, adzes	grizzly bears, California poppies, truffles, protozoa	house cats, Dolly the sheep, GMO corn, Bourbon roses	Spinuzzi's traffic engineers, Miettinen's scientists, ANT's princes	World Trade Organization, ISO, Doctors without Borders, United Nations
Conditional agency	Produce effects	+	+	+	+	+	+
Need-based agency	Act according to own biological needs	–	–	+	+	+	–
Need-based agency	Act according to own cultural needs	–	–	–	–	+	+
Delegated agency	Realize intentions of (other) human beings	–	+	–	+	+	+

Table 3.1: Forms of agency

Living beings are a special kind of agent in striving to meet needs in the world, engaging other entities as they do so in a patterned way. A plant with its biological needs reaches for the sun, produces chlorophyll. Its flowers attract bees of a particular kind, its seeds are eaten by certain birds who scatter them in the woods.

Leontiev searched for a concept to describe the context in which mind evolved, considering "life," but rejecting it as too general. He settled on activity, defining it in terms of a subject's relation to a world in which it attempts to fulfill its needs. Non-living things are inert in not having needs. Phenomenologists have also noticed this, observing that things do not "care" as Heidegger (1962) proposed. Subjects engage in activity because they care about what will happen to them in the future (see also Emirbayer and Mische, 1998). This caring is the condition of the tiniest one-celled animal struggling for a mite of algae, to humans attempting to solve the most difficult scientific or social problems. In her novel *Housekeeping*, Marilynne Robinson (1980) put it poetically: "And there is no living creature, though the whims of eons have put its eyes on boggling stalks and clamped it in a carapace, diminished it to a pinpoint and given it a taste for mud and stuck it down a well or hid it under a stone, but that creature will live on if it can."

Agency should not be considered a monolithic property that is either categorically present or absent. Producing effects, acting, and realizing intentions, while potentialities of certain kinds of agents, vary within the enactment of a specific activity. Extending the notion of agency beyond human subjects may appear a deviation from the asymmetry of the subject and the object endorsed by activity theory. However, we propose a combination of (1) a strict subject-object dichotomy (and resulting asymmetry) and (2) the notion of levels of agency, that is, understanding agency as a dimension rather than a binary attribute.

With this in mind, we can differentiate between types, or levels of agency. Our analysis, as depicted in Table 3.1, includes:

Need-based agency. Human beings have both biological and cultural needs. To meet their needs they form intentions and act on the intentions. Similar types of agency are manifested by social entities (even though they do not have biological needs) and higher animals (even though they do not have cultural needs).

Delegated agency. Various things and living beings can be said to realize intentions, but these intentions are delegated by somebody or something else. For example, when winning a race, a race horse realizes the intentions of its breeders. At other times, though, the horse realizes its own intentions—grazing in the pasture or resting in its stall. Human society is organized such that humans delegate the actions needed to realize intentions to other humans. Sometimes the subject receiving the delegated intentions accepts them as her own, and other times she carries out the necessary actions based on her own different intentions. Marx's notion of "alienated labor" is the classic case of separating a subject's actions on behalf of someone else and her own intentions. The worker performs the actions to receive a wage but has no interest in, for example, the quality of a product save as it affects her wage.

Conditional agency. Anything and anyone can produce unintended effects. The Russian winter of 1812 did not target Napoleon's army but undoubtedly contributed to its defeat. Truck drivers do not intend to create obstacles on highways but they repeatedly do. Even without having an intention, something or somebody may constitute a force—or condition—to be reckoned with.

ARTIFACTS

Artifacts are special agents that are the product of cultural needs. Humans have gained some control over our needs through the design and deployment of artifacts that embody our intentions and desires. We are able, in the lifetime of a single individual, to create new solutions to meet needs as conditions change. As we saw in Chapter 2, artifacts empower people through the use of technical and psychological tools. Activity theory conceptualizes the potency of human agency in part through the principle of mediation: tools empower in mediating between people and the world. People "appropriate" tools in order to empower themselves to fulfill their objects (Wertsch, 1998). The principle of mediation clearly indicates that things have agency, because if they did not, they could not act as mediators. In a vivid historical example, Zinchenko (1996) observed, "Communist and fascist symbols acquired such fanatic energy that . . . they nearly devoured the great cultures of Russia and Germany."

Functional organs are a special kind of mediator. Zinchenko (1996) discussed the cellist Rostropovich and the quality of mediation provided by his cello. When asked in an interview about his relationship to his cello, Rostropovich replied:

There no longer exist relations between us. Some time ago I lost my sense of the border between us. . . . In a portrait [by the painter Glikman] . . . there I was—and my cello became just a red spot at my belly . . . (quoted in Zinchenko, 1996).

A functional organ is a different relation between human and thing than nodes in an actor-network (see Latour, 1993). A functional organ brings human and thing closely together, in a relation more intimate than a system of like nodes. A red spot at the belly is an apt metaphor for how we experience our most cherished technologies. As noted in Chapter 2, functional organs are subsystems that are integral parts of a subject who still decides when to use functional organs and whether they have to be altered or even abandoned.

Actor-network theory speaks of artifacts as having "delegated competences" (Latour, 1993). Interests are "translated" between elements in the network, that is, performances and competences move back and forth between nodes in a symmetrical network. For example, a user's competence at typing URLs can be translated to a computer which can guess at the character string intended by the user, if a few clues are provided, and thereby complete the typing for the user.

In the scheme proposed in Table 3.1, delegation flows from humans to the other kinds of agents (including other humans). But in actor-network theory a non-human entity might delegate to a human. So a cell phone demands fresh batteries. It enlists the human to replace batteries by beeping when the batteries are low. In activity theory, there is no delegation from thing to human; the human decides that in order to use the mediating technology, she will supply the batteries. The human has other possibilities. She can turn off the beeper, or can throw away the cell phone, or seek out a new cell phone with superior battery technology. At any time she can resist; she can modify; she can alter her relationship to the technology based on her intentions. The cell phone, by contrast, does what it was programmed to do; it is without desire or intention. The cell phone's agency is manifest in its ability to beep but it is an agency designed and delegated by humans.

Artifacts can be designed to produce effects to replace human labor at the level of operations and actions. Leontiev (1978) observed that operations are destined to become functions of machines, and indeed the proliferation of such machines created since the Industrial Revolution has continued unabated (as the Luddites also foresaw). Automatic gearboxes, electric mixers, dishwashers, and text completion are examples of artifacts taking on some tedious operations.

At the level of actions, programmable artifacts have proved efficient and even intelligent. As early as the beginning of the 19th century, Jacquard looms driven by punched cards created elaborate fabrics (and provided the inspiration for the design of Babbage's Analytical Engine as well as Hollerith's Census Machine used to conduct the U.S. Census in 1890). A modern washing machine can carry out an impressive sequence of actions. And of course computers are the exemplar of programmable artifacts, interpreting languages that permit flexible sequences of actions (and operations) on a new scale of complexity.

While mediators can be designed to autonomously assume human operations and actions, they cannot, in themselves, create meaningful activities. Artifacts cannot decide what they want, they cannot form an intention, or say what is meaningful and what is not.

Though we can't think of any actual artifacts with intention or desire, such artifacts are alive and well in the human consciousness. The Golem, Frankenstein's monster, the robot Maria in Lang's Metropolis, HAL in 2001, and the Terminator, to name a few, inhabit a narrative universe in which cyborgian desires exert powerful influences in human life. These humanoid characters, while compelling, appear to be rather obvious projections of human desires and fears. A more likely source of artifacts with intention may be research in artificial life, an area to which we will look for interesting future developments (Reynolds, 1987).

Mediators empower in ways specified by human designers, but the agency of artifacts may also be conditional, producing unintended effects. Winner (1977; 1986) has explored the unintended consequences of technology in several empirical investigations. Shaffer and Clinton (2006) pointed to the studies of Postman (1993) and Tenner (1997) in observing that "[things] have a way of exceeding or changing the designs of their makers." Unintended consequences of artifacts may be of value to people (such as the discovery of penicillin) or they may be tragic (such as an explosion at a nuclear power plant).

CONCLUSION

We identified different kinds of agents according to whether they are driven by the demands of life and whether they embody cultural needs. Table 3.1 suggests an interesting tension. Every agent is capable of producing effects for which there is no intention. The more cultural things (living and non-living) we have in the world, things that appear as a result of human design and intention, the more possibilities we introduce for conditional agency, that is, for new kinds of unintended effects.

CHAPTER 4

Activity and experience

INTRODUCTION

Having examined the fundamental principles of activity theory and reflected on their relation to the concept of agency, we move to another notion popular in HCI discourse: experience. We analyze what experience might mean for HCI using activity theory as a lens. Experience was an essential aspect of the formulation of the earliest questions that drove activity theory. The very rationale for employing activity as a foundational concept in Leontiev's framework was an attempt to resolve a common dilemma faced by most psychological theories, that is, the need to choose between two mutually exclusive objectives: (a) providing a rich and nuanced understanding of mental phenomena and subjective experience, and (b) establishing psychology as a field of "truly scientific" research, based on rigorous methods and conceptually consistent with the bodies of knowledge accumulated in other sciences such as biology.

As the history of psychology shows, these two objectives are difficult to combine. Detailed studies of subjective human experiences often lack rigor and reliability, while natural science-style approaches (e.g., behaviorism) are often reductionist in the sense that they effectively exclude the mind as such from their definition of the object of psychological study (and, instead, study something else, e.g., behavior). According to Leontiev, using activity as a basic category of psychological analysis opens up a possibility to develop a new type of psychological theory which would combine the rigor of natural sciences with a non-reductionist perspective on human mind.

Building on Rubinshtein's principle of the "unity and inseparability of consciousness and activity"(Rubinshtein, 1946), Leontiev introduced object-oriented activity as a unit of analysis in psychology in order to define the context within which mental processes and subjective phenomena emerge and acquire their meaning. The context of activity, therefore, should be analyzed to properly understand the nature of subjective phenomena. This strategy was considered a way to ensure that human experience would remain an object of psychological study (and not be "reduced away"), while providing a solid basis for its systematic, rigorous, scientific analysis.

The underlying idea of Leontiev's project in psychology as a whole was to study mental processes as an inherent, organic, and necessary facet of activity, that is, need-based, object-oriented interaction between the subject and the world. Recognizing mental processes and subjective experiences as an essential aspect of an activity meant that they were considered as embedded in a system of causal relations within the activity, rather than as merely epiphenomena, a "shadow" of other processes that actually determine the course of the activity. Conceiving psychological phenomena as embedded in activity also meant that the main aim of psychological analysis should be to understand the specific role and place of subjective phenomena in activity as a whole.

Very roughly, the research program undertaken to complete Leontiev's project can be broken down into three more specific lines of study, each having its own objective. First, it was necessary to elaborate the concept of activity, specify the meaning of the concept, and develop an analytical framework that would support concrete studies of particular activities. The second objective was to investigate two-way causal interrelationships between mental processes and other ("non-psychological") facets of activity, and understand the relations underlying their mutual impacts and transformations. Third, attaining the first two objectives would constitute prerequisites for achieving the aim of advancing theoretical and empirical exploration into traditional problems of psychology and providing new insights into the nature and variety of mental processes and subjective phenomena.

The outcomes of pursuing these three objectives were quite different in terms of their relative success. The first line of exploration can be considered highly successful. The concept of activity as being object-oriented, purposeful, mediated, hierarchically organized, social, and developing, was, either wholly or partly adopted in a wide range of studies in various disciplines. Most notably, it was the main inspiration for the development of Engeström's activity system model (Engeström, 1987).

The work along the second line of explorations can be qualified as generally successful. As discussed in Chapter 2, a number of important and influential insights about how the structure and dynamics of activity are related to subjective phenomena were formulated in activity theory. These insights were based on ideas which were both adopted from Vygotsky (e.g., internalization) and Rubinshtein (e.g., unity and inseparability of consciousness and activity) and developed by Leontiev himself (e.g., the structural similarity of internal and external activities). The impact of these insights was, however, somewhat more limited than that of Leontiev's framework for the analysis of the structure and basic properties of activity.

The overall impact of the third line of exploration, however, appears to be not as significant as the impact of the first two. Experimental and conceptual studies of specific mental processes and subjective phenomena, conducted by Leontiev, are generally less known and less influential compared to his theoretical work focusing on the concept of activity and the relationship between activity and mind. With some notable exceptions (e.g., Cole, 1996; Wertsch, 1998), activity theory has not been used outside Russia as a framework for psychological studies of mental phenomena. For the most part, when used internationally, activity theory was adopted in other areas than psychology (e.g., CRADLE, Center for Research on Activity, Development and Learning, n.d.), and the specifically psychological aspects of the theory were often "lost in translation" as less relevant to the concerns of a respective area.

The selective adoption of activity theory concepts has also been the case in the field of HCI. When the theory was introduced as a conceptual foundation for the second-wave, "post-cognitivist HCI" (Bødker, 1991; see also Kaptelinin et al., 2003), it was found relevant and useful for HCI research mostly because it brought in the concepts of tool mediation and the hierarchical structure of activity, and because it emphasized the centrality of social context and development. These ideas were taken up owing to their relevance to second-wave HCI which was essentially concerned with understanding—and addressing—the needs for creating technological support for purposeful, mostly work-related, activities. Activity-theoretical analyses of mental processes and phenomena, such as sensation, perception, memory, and consciousness, were largely left out during the adoption as less relevant.

However, recently the concerns and priorities of HCI research have undergone significant changes. The importance of understanding subjective phenomena which are induced by, or otherwise related to, the use of digital technologies, has become a central issue in HCI. In the last decade conceptual frameworks specifically dealing with subjective phenomena such as emotional design (Norman, 2004) and technology as experience (McCarthy and Wright, 2004), have emerged. The concept of "experience" has become an increasingly important object of research in conceptual explorations (Forlizzi and Battarbee, 2004), experimental studies (Hassenzahl, 2003), and practice (Buchenau and Suri, 2000). At the time of this writing, "experience" is one of the most common terms in the field and, in a sense, an emblem of current HCI. The recently established "Human Centered Informatics" series, of which this book is a part, already features several recent titles on "experience" and "engagement." The theme of the CHI 2012 Conference was "It's the experience"[7]. A recent CHI paper is entirely devoted to a bibliographic analysis of empirical HCI research on experience (Bargas-Avila and Hornbacck, 2011).

These ongoing changes in the scope and foci of HCI research and practice mean that the theoretical needs of the field are changing. While understanding the structure and dynamics of purposeful human activities and identifying possibilities for their advanced technological support remain important issues, there is currently also marked interest in frameworks that can provide an explanation of why and how certain subjective phenomena are taking place in situations surrounding the use of interactive technologies. In line with this current trend, in this chapter we discuss the potential of activity theory as a conceptual tool for analyzing experience in the context of HCI.

ANALYSES OF SUBJECTIVE PHENOMENA IN ACTIVITY THEORY

Analysis of subjective experiences was a major concern in the work of Vygotsky and Rubinshtein, the two psychologists who made the most substantial impact on Leontiev's activity theory. Vygotsky (1978) was especially interested in how people acquire the meaning of culturally developed semiotic systems, and emphasized the central role of social interactions in the process. In a voluminous (but still unfinished) manuscript, entitled "The teaching of emotions," Vygotsky criticized the prevalence of Cartesian mind-body dualism in psychological theories of emotions of that time and called for bringing in non-Cartesian philosophical perspectives (he specifically mentioned Spinoza), that would allow psychologists to analyze different aspects of emotions, such as subjective phenomena and physiological processes, within a single coherent framework (Vygotsky, 1983).

In line with his principle of unity and inseparability of consciousness and activity, Rubinshtein (1946) maintained that experience should not be separated from action. He observed that

Those who deliberately look for experience, find emptiness. But let a person immerse himself in an action—a deep, real-life action—and he will be flooded with experience. [. . .] Experience is both a result and prerequisite of action, either internal or external. Mutually interpenetrating and supporting one another, they constitute a true unity, two interrelated sides of the coherent whole, – that is, human life and activity.

Leontiev himself can be credited with the development of several concepts intended to explain the nature of certain mental phenomena. In his analysis of the emergence of psyche in biological evolution he proposed that the first, most elementary subjective phenomenon, that of sensation, is directly linked to the ability of an organism to react to signals. By signals he meant those stimuli which are not in themselves important for the survival of the organism, but indicate the presence of important stimuli (e.g., the smell of food indicates that food might be around).

Another idea, first expressed as early as in the 1940s (Leontiev, 1944), was that there is a causal link between the structure of activity and the content of consciousness. More specifically, it was posited that people are conscious of the objects at which their activity is immediately directed at a certain moment. For instance, if a student writes an essay and concentrates on how to formulate an idea, she is aware of the idea, but not the spelling of the words she is writing. When the focus of activity changes (e.g., to checking the essay for typos), the content of consciousness changes accordingly.

A wide range of activity-theoretical studies, conducted by both Leontiev and other Russian psychologists, dealt with perception. Perception was understood as an active process carried out through "perceptual actions and operations" directed at the object of perception. Leontiev proposed the "replication" (or "likening") hypothesis to explain how perceptual actions may contribute to the development of the image of an object. According to this hypothesis, external components of perception, such as eye movements (in the case of vision) or hand movements (in the case of haptic perception) in the process of exploring an object become adjusted to an object's properties (e.g., follow its shape) and in doing so produce an "imprint," if an imprecise one, of the object, which serves as a representation of the object in the perceptual system. This hypothesis was tested in experiments in which Leontiev and his colleagues attempted (and succeeded) to form perfect pitch in children by having the participants not only differentiate, but also vocalize sounds of different pitch (Leontiev, 1981).

As noted in Chapter 2, activity theory understands emotions as direct indicators of the status of an activity as a whole. Objects or events that have or may potentially have significant impact, either positive or negative, on attaining the motive of an activity are "marked" by emotions, to make sure a swift action can be taken, if necessary. Emotions do not disclose the reasons why they occur, so sometimes people do not easily understand why they experience a certain emotion.

Since human actions are often poly-motivated, people may experience unanticipated or mixed emotions if the outcome of an action is positively related to one of its motives but negatively related to another one. Leontiev (1978) illustrates this situation with the example of a "bitter candy." He describes a study in which children were rewarded with a candy for successfully solving the experimental task. One participant cheated to get the reward, and she received the candy. However, the candy did not make her happy. Instead, the girl broke in tears when she got it.

The most explicit and systematic attempt to provide an activity-theoretical account of subjective experiences was made by Leontiev (1978) in his notion of the structure of individual consciousness. Leontiev identified three key components of consciousness: meaning, personal meaning, and the "sensorial fabrics of consciousness." Meanings are the standard, socially shared meanings of objects and events which we need to understand in order to communicate with other people. Personal meanings are the ways socially shared meanings are related to our motives, goals, hopes, and fears. Finally, the "sensorial fabrics of consciousness" are the images brought to us by our senses.

During the last years of his life, Leontiev was working on the development of an activity theoretical account of how the world is subjectively experienced by human beings in their everyday life. This work remained unfinished. A sketch of some of his ideas about the "image of the world" is presented in a posthumous article entitled "The psychology of image"(Leontiev, 1979).

Therefore, over time activity theory has developed a number of concepts and hypotheses about the nature of subjective experiences and their relationship with the objective conditions of human life and activity. For various reasons, however, the potential of these analytical tools has not been fully exploited in concrete studies of mental phenomena.

ACTIVITY THEORETICAL VS. PHENOMENOLOGICAL PERSPECTIVES IN HCI

The turn to experience in HCI can be directly linked to the changing practices of the use and design of interactive technologies in society at large. Over the last decade or two, interactive technologies have become ordinary consumer products, not bound to predetermined workplace contexts. Therefore, purchasing decisions are increasingly determined not only by the functionality of a product but by other factors as well, such as appearance, prestige, and so on (Nelson and Stolterman, 2003). In many popular niches (mobile phones, cameras, laptops, tablets) a variety of available products provide more or less the same functionality, so consumers can choose a product by taking into account their personal preferences and the prospective context (or contexts) of use. The success or failure of a product critically depends not only on its utility and usability, but also on whether or not customers like the product (or even more so, whether or not they like it more than other competing products). Therefore, it is critically important to understand how to design interactive products that ensure "good user experience." The practical importance of developing a thorough understanding of the meaning of user experience and ways to support it with appropriate designs has been, arguably, a key motivation behind the growing interest in "experience" in recent HCI research.

Kuutti (2010) observes that HCI studies of user experience are for the most part empirical, with relatively little focus on theory. More efforts are invested in collecting and generalizing empirical evidence with the aim of operationalizing the concept of experience (e.g., identifying different attributes and dimensions) compared to attempts to understand the meaning of the concept and its place within a larger conceptual framework. While acknowledging the importance of empirical studies, Kuutti concludes his reflections on the prevalence of purely empirical studies of experience in nowadays HCI by saying:

. . . I feel that there should also be a complementary conceptual and theoretical debate on the issue, and this is currently lacking.

According to Kuutti (2010), post-cognitivist HCI theoretical frameworks, including anthropological, phenomenological, and activity-theoretical ones, should all be contributing to conceptual explorations of experience. We concur with Kuutti that the grand challenge of understanding experience in the context of HCI requires a joint large-scale investigation, conducted from multiple theoretical perspectives. In what follows we tentatively explore the prospects of how activity theory can contribute to such a collaborative effort. In order to do so we contrast activity theory to phenomenology, a theoretical approach that guides much of current HCI research on experience. The discussion below builds on our previous analysis (Kaptelinin and Nardi, 2006) and specifically deals with phenomenologically inspired HCI research (e.g., Dourish, 2001; Fällman, 2003; Svanaes, 2000) rather than phenomenology in general.

As we argued elsewhere (Kaptelinin and Nardi, 2006), there are many deep conceptual similarities between activity theory and phenomenology. Like other post-cognitivist theories such as distributed cognition (e.g., Hollan et al., 2000) and actor-network theory (e.g., Callon, 1986), they are highly critical of Cartesian mind-body dualism and maintain that there is a fundamental unity of the mind and the world. Another basic idea shared by most post-cognitivist theories is that technology plays a vital role in human life.

In addition, both activity theory (Leontiev's version) and phenomenology, as opposed to some other post-cognitivist theories, are primarily interested in individual subjects. While distributed cognition and actor-network theory, each in its particular way, define their objects of analysis in terms of supra-individual entities (respectively, information-processing units comprising people and artifacts, and actor networks) activity theory and phenomenology retain a commitment to the individual subject.

For them [i.e., activity theory and phenomenology] contextual analysis is a way to reach a deeper understanding of individual human beings (Kaptelinin and Nardi, 2006).

One more common feature of activity theory and phenomenology is that they both describe subjective experience in terms of meaning. Dourish (2001) identifies three components of meaning: ontology, intentionality, and inter-subjectivity. These components cannot be directly mapped to Leontiev's three facets of consciousness, described above (meaning, personal meaning, and the sensorial fabric of consciousness) but the emphasis on different aspects of meaning is apparent in both cases.

Despite these similarities, activity theory and phenomenology are different in a number of important respects. The most obvious difference is that activity theory is at its roots a psychological approach, while phenomenology is a philosophical one. This raises the intriguing question of whether or not it is possible at all to systematically compare these approaches. Would it be comparing apples and oranges? In our view, there are some reasons for caution, since the approaches represent different types of inquiry and are developed within different traditions. However, we argue that the theories can be meaningfully compared. Each theory has close connections to both philosophy and psychology. Activity theory are heavily influenced by German philosophy, primarily that of Marx and Hegel. Phenomenology's pedigree can be traced to psychology—in particular,

Brentano's "act psychology"(Brentano, 1987)—which was one of the main influences behind the very emergence of phenomenology. Therefore, activity theory and phenomenology represent, respectively, a philosophically inspired psychological approach and a psychologically inspired philosophical approach. There are thus reasons to believe they are similar enough to allow meaningful comparison.

A substantial difference between activity theory and phenomenology lies in their respective conceptual points of departure. Activity theory understands subjects as constituted by their inherently social activities that transform both subjects and the world (objects). Activities, therefore, set subjects apart and, at the same time, relate them to the world. Since subjects have need-based agency and become what they are through their socially and physically distributed activities, a detailed account of motivation, development, and social-cultural context is a necessary precondition for understanding subjects, their "acting-in-the world." In phenomenology, subjects are also assumed to be one with the world—their very existence is defined as "being-in-the world"(Heidegger, 1962). However, the most fundamental issue to be explored is formulated in phenomenology in terms of how people make sense of their existence and how the world reveals itself to subjects. The issue of how subjects come to exist in the first place is not systematically analyzed, and neither are the specific needs and goals underlying the active, engaged nature of "being-in-the-world." In addition, while the importance of the social context was recognized (and reflected), for instance in the Heidegger's notion of "being with," which was mentioned, but not elaborated upon (Polt, 1999), it did not become a central issue in the phenomenological tradition until the notion of intersubjectivity was introduced to phenomenology discourse (see Dourish, 2001).

These general theoretical differences between activity theory and phenomenology imply that their perspectives on experience do not coincide. Some disparities are discussed below in relation to the notion of embodiment.

Embodied interaction is a phenomenologically inspired concept in HCI proposed by Dourish (2001) (and expressed in somewhat different ways by other researchers, as well). The underlying idea is that analysis and design of interactive technologies should be based on the understanding of human beings as entities that have physical and social attributes (i.e., "bodies") and are engaged in interaction with other entities in their physical and social environments. The concept of embodied interaction was taken up in HCI and interaction design, especially interpreted in a literal sense, as dealing with human bodies—that is, taking into account the human body in analysis, design, and use of technology (e.g., Hornecker and Buur, 2006; Klemmer et al., 2006).

Baumer and Tomlinson (2011) observed: "While theoretically plausible, most traditional accounts of AT [activity theory] and DCog [distributed cognition] do not include the body as a mediating tool or as a representational medium." We concur with both claims. We agree that the role of body in human interaction with the world has not been an object of systematic analysis in activity-theoretical research, and we also agree that such analysis is theoretically plausible. In our view, some ideas of activity theory can be fruitfully applied in HCI to provide new insights about physical embodiment. In particular, activity theory suggests that exploring new opportunities for technological support of physically embodied interaction should not be limited to understanding the needs and capabilities of our "natural" bodies (even though that is also important). The capabilities of our "natural" bodies, generally speaking, do not directly determine how we interact with our physical environments. The capabilities of our bodies are extended with artifacts, and our extended bodies open new horizons of physical interaction with the world, such as moving in space at the speed of 200 km/hour (body extended with a car) or jumping off a high cliff (body extended with a hang glider). The risk of focusing too much on natural bodies can be illustrated by the amazing accomplishments, both physical (e.g., the Paralympics) and intellectual, achieved by some people with severe physical disabilities. Therefore, the human body in a broad sense should be considered as dynamic and developing. Of course the limitations of our "natural" bodies should be seriously taken into account when designing technology-rich environments. We would argue, however, that it is equally important to explore possibilities for designing "extended bodies" rather than merely adapting the environment to our current limitations.

Let us give a simple example illustrating our point. If someone's sight is not 20-20, there are two ways to help: change the environment to adjust it to the limited capabilities of the person (e.g., increase the font size of the text presented on an electronic display) or choose appropriate eyeglasses or lenses to correct the person's vision. In both cases one needs to examine the person's sight, but in somewhat different ways. In our view, currently the studies of physical embodiment in HCI tend to adopt the first of these approaches, while we believe that both approaches are important and need to be explored in the field.

In this section we claimed that activity theory and phenomenology have much in common, but that they have radically different conceptual points of departure. Are we contradicting ourselves? Not really. Even though activity theory and phenomenology do differ in their basic perspectives, the directions of their development seem to point in the same general direction. Activity theory starts with an analysis of the structure and dynamics of social, mediated, purposeful activity, and aims to eventually use it as a basis for revealing the richness of human experience. For phenomenology the starting point is the richness of human experience, to understand which the notions of being-in-the-world, equipment, and intersubjectivity were introduced at various stages of post-Husserlian development of the tradition (Dourish, 2001; Svanaes, 2000). In our view, over time activity theory and phenomenology have become closer to one another, even though this similarity is sometimes difficult to discern. Of course, the approaches remain different, and they will always be. But the discussion in this section suggests that in analysis of the complex phenomena of human uses of technology, HCI has no choice but to address the fundamental issues of meaning, value, identity, and justice (as discussed in the concluding chapter of this book), and activity theory and phenomenology (as well as, probably, other approaches) can be coordinated within a larger scale theoretical inquiry.

[7]http://chi2012.acm.org/.

CHAPTER 5

Activity-centric computing

Moving beyond discussion of theoretical precepts, we consider a body of HCI work that takes "activity" as a grounding orientation. This work grows out of dissatisfaction with the prevailing application-centric view of computing in which it is up to the user to manage a set of individual applications largely ignorant of one another. Even operations as simple as cut and paste do not always work fluidly across different applications (for example the user may have to take steps to harmonize fonts and other formatting once a "paste" has been made, or it may be impossible to paste an item at all). Applications have little idea what a user has been doing and how they might, collectively, help. For example, when adding email attachments, the most logical folder choice is the one the user was most recently working in. But most mailers offer an unchanging generic choice.

While the importance of supporting meaningful human activities may seem obvious, the rationale behind the design of many existing systems reflects engineering priorities (it is easier to design applications without rich knowledge of other applications). However, from the user's perspective, this approach has a major drawback: when applied in the design of digital environments, it results in fragmented workspaces. Users often need to combine several applications to complete a task: for instance, one may use a web browser to get access to online resources, a word processor to compose a document, and an email program to send the document to a colleague or client. As a result, the user has to deal with several types of information objects: web pages, documents, email messages, and so on (Kaptelinin and Czerwinski, 2007). Desktop systems provide some support for integrating diverse information objects such as displaying objects in windows that share the same screen space and can be managed—moved, resized, closed —in a uniform way. But the support is limited. Apart from some cross-application shortcuts (such as opening a website in a browser by clicking its

URL in a text document), the user must find and handle information objects of different types separately, even if these objects are directly relevant to the task at hand and closely related to one another (Bardram et al., 2006; Kaptelinin, 1996a). The lack of cross-tool (cf. Boardman and Sasse, 2004) integration is especially evident when the user wants to save all task-related information objects, such as documents, email messages, and URLs, as a single archive. The functionality of a typical desktop system is not sufficient to achieve that in a simple and straightforward way. Instead, the user must devise a workaround (e.g., copy URLs and messages to a document and then save all task-related documents in a separate folder).

A HISTORICAL ACCOUNT OF ACTIVITY-CENTRIC COMPUTING

The limitations of application-centric computing were recognized early in the history of HCI research, and a number of alternative underlying principles for digital work environments have been proposed (Kaptelinin and Czerwinski, 2007). One of the ideas, explored in several research and development projects over the past few decades, was organizing digital resources around meaningful, higher level tasks of the user—that is, the idea of "activity-centric computing." One of the oldest such designs, and still admirable, was the ROOMS system which divided the digital workspace of a desktop into special-purpose sub-areas or "rooms," each dedicated to a certain type of activity and each furnished with customized sets of tools necessary to carry out the activity (Card and Henderson, 1987; Henderson and Card, 1986). The design of ROOMS was influenced by research carried out by Don Norman's group at the University of California, San Diego, in which special attention was paid to how technology users switch between multiple activities (Bannon et al., 1983; Cypher, 1986).

As originally designed it was not widely used, but similar solutions based on the same idea, known as "virtual desktops," have been implemented in a number of systems such as X window managers (Windows Managers for X). ROOMs also influenced the conceptual design of the Personal Role Manager which aimed at supporting switching between a user's different roles by providing selective access to collections of resources associated with each of the roles (Plaisant and Shneiderman, 1994).

While the ROOMS system and the Personal Role Manager suggested certain ways to alleviate problems with application-centric computing, they did not go far enough to offer a general alternative to that approach. Such an alternative, named Activity-Based Computing (ABC), was proposed by Norman and his colleagues at Apple Computer in the 1990s (Norman, 1998). The key aim of ABC was to make sure that the user gains access to resources necessary to carry out the activity at hand with little or no overhead and minimal interference with other activities. This aim was to be achieved by organizing various types of resources into activity-specific "packages" supporting quick and easy switching between activities, and by hiding unrelated items. Making it all possible required deep changes in the computer industry's approach to the development of interactive technologies and, in particular, abandoning the application-centric perspective.

According to Norman, it was not possible, for various reasons, to achieve such a change in industry's perspective at that time (Norman, 1998). But even though the immediate aims of the ABC initiative at Apple Computer were not attained, the underlying ideas made a substantial impact on work in activity-centric computing. In his more recent work Norman himself returns to activity-based notions and argues that limitations of traditional human-centered design can be overcome by adopting an activity-centric approach (Norman, 2005, 2006).

In the last decade or so the number of systems and frameworks falling in the general category of "activity-centric computing" has significantly increased. The Task Gallery (Robertson et al., 2000) visualizes a collection of task-specific workspaces as canvases hanging on the walls of a corridor. The Kimura system (Voida et al., 2002, 2007) combines activity-specific virtual desktops with an advanced overview of all ongoing activities of a user. The system employs a large surface view (e.g., an image projected on the office walls) to display a set of specially created, customized images for each of the background activities of the user to represent the key objects and current status of an activity. The images are dynamic; they automatically visualize relevant processes and events, such as a document being printed or a colleague becoming available for a face-to-face meeting. Work on the Kimura system fed into the development of another activity-centric system, Giornata, a personal computer environment in which a virtual desktop is set up for each new activity (Voida and Mynatt, 2009).

The UMEA (User-Monitoring Environments for Activities) system (Kaptelinin, 2003) monitors user actions and automatically creates organized sets of pointers to various information objects (e.g., documents, web pages, or contacts) employed by the user when working on the currently active higher-level task (or "project"). When the user switches between projects there is no need to search for relevant resources if they were already found before. The user immediately gets access to the project-specific lists of resources which are automatically created by the system. The TaskTracer system (Dragunov et al., 2005) aims to provide a similar kind of support, but the lists of resources are identified by analyzing the history of user actions and making inferences about the items to include in a task-specific list rather than by relying on the user's explicit selection of a certain task as "active." Another approach to task management was implemented in the TaskMaster system (Bellotti et al., 2003). The system extends a conventional email program by adding a new type of information object, "thrasks," a cross of "threads" and "tasks." A thrask includes all task-related email messages, a rich source of task-related resources if a substantial part of project management takes place in email. TaskMaster also allows the user to add to thrasks other types of information objects such as documents, and provides some personal information management functionality.

Several systems which do not explicitly adopt an activity-centric perspective can also be considered relevant. The underlying idea of the Lifestreams system (Freeman and Gelernter, 2007) is to organize all information objects in a user's personal information space in a chronological order and provide advanced tools for "extracting" subsets of the whole sequence—or "sub-streams"—depending on the user's current needs. The sub-streams can be understood as digital traces of unfolding activities, so that specifying sub-streams can be considered a particular case of specifying certain activity contexts. The ContactMap system (Nardi et al., 2002) organizes information objects available to a user of a desktop environment around the user's contacts, that is, people with whom the user is communicating or collaborating. Since activities, or groups of activities, can often be defined by specifying other people involved, the structure of an individual ContactMap desktop indirectly reflects the structure of user's activities in general. The WorkspaceMirror system (Boardman and Sasse, 2004) addresses one of the most salient problems with application-centric computer environment, the fragmentation caused by multiple information hierarchies such as a file system, email mailboxes, and web browsers' "favorites." The WorkspaceMirror supports maintaining a consistent information structure across several hierarchies, and thus alleviates fragmentation. Even though WorkspaceMirror does not provide a complete alternative to application-centric computing, it does take a step toward creating more activity-centric workspaces by supporting the integration of various types of information objects necessary to carry out the task at hand. The GroupBar and Elastic Fabrics systems (Robertson et al., 2007), enable grouping together diverse types of information objects by, respectively, integrating several tiles in a Windows Task Bar into a single unit (GroupBar) and moving progressively diminishing images of information objects from the center to the periphery of the user's work area. These techniques allow for creating project-specific collections of resources and managing entire collections when switching between activities.

Explorations into activity-centric computing in the last decade were not limited to individual systems. Several research programs, each comprising a range of empirical studies and technological developments, dealt with activity-centric computing, most notably Project Aura at Carnegie Mellon University (Sousa and Garlan, 2001), the Unified Activity Management at IBM Research (Millen et al., 2005; Moran, 2005a,b; Moran et al., 2005; Muller et al., 2004) and the Activity-Based Computing (ABC) project at the IT University of Copenhagen (Bardram, 2005; Bardram et al., 2006; Bardram, 2007, 2009; Christensen and Bardram, 2002).

Project Aura aims to develop a context-aware technology that would act "on behalf of a user to manage resources, provide continuity, and support high-level user tasks" by taking into account the users' context (e.g., location), tasks, and preferences (Sousa and Garlan, 2001). The objective of the Unified Activity Management project is to use explicit representations of human activities to develop work support systems that would allow people to successfully manage—that is, set up, prioritize, coordinate, and execute—individual and collective activities. "Activity" is understood in a broad sense as "any coherent set of actions that we take towards some end, be it specific or vague" (Unified Activity Management). Explicit representations of both formal and informal work processes within uniform activity structures (consisting, e.g., of a description of sub-activities such as resources, deadlines, and dependencies), are envisioned as activity management tools that would guide and support rather than control and constrain their users. Such representations, integrated with potentially needed resources, are expected to help organize work processes around activities rather than tools or other artifacts. A collection of activity structures presented in a consistent way would make it possible for a person or group to manage the whole range of their activities. Finally, an important advantage of explicit representations of activities is claimed to be a support for the evolutionary development of activities over time through specifying recurrent patterns of activities (Activity Patterns) and making cumulative improvements in the patterns (Moran, 2005a,b; Moran et al., 2005). The work within this project, as well as its companion Activity Explorer, resulted in the development of tools such as Activity Tableau and empirical studies of people working over extended periods of time in activity-centric environments (Balakrishnan et al., 2010; Millen et al., 2005; Muller et al., 2004).

Jacob Bardram and his colleagues address the issue of how to support mobility and collaboration in human work activities in their work on Activity-based Computing (Bardram, 2005; Bardram et al., 2006; Bardram, 2007; Christensen and Bardram, 2002). The solution explored within the project is to break away from traditional application- and document-centric computing and make computational activities, understood as aggregations of "services, resources, artifacts, and users that are relevant for a real world human activity," first-class entities, explicitly represented in computer systems (Bardram, 2009). It is argued that a computer infrastructure that would make it possible for users to discover, create, suspend, save, and otherwise manage computational activities should be based on the following principles: (a) activity-centered resource aggregation (integrating diverse resources needed to carry out an activity), (b) activity suspension and resumption (providing means for handling activity switching and interruptions), (c) activity roaming (providing consistent support for activities, which unfold across different contexts and are carried out with different computing technologies), (d) activity sharing (supporting collaboration), and (e) activity awareness (making a system "aware" of the current real-life context of the user) (Bardram, 2009). It should be specifically emphasized that the core principles refer to computational activities which should not be confused with human activities. As Bardram (2005) explains, a computational activity

. . . does not model nor control real-world human activities. A computational activity can be created and modified according to the desire of the user, and does not come from models of work activities.

Bardram's approach has been applied in the development of a number of concrete technologies. A range of technologies have been designed to support collaborative, mobile work of medical personnel in hospital environments (Activity-Based Computing, n.d.). In addition, the approach has also been implemented in the design of the Windows XP ABC system, embedded in a conventional personal computing environment.

ACTIVITY-CENTRIC COMPUTING AND ACTIVITY THEORY

As follows from the historical analysis in the previous section, activity-centric computing is a general approach pursued from a variety of different perspectives. Activity theory has been one such perspective—a number of research and development explorations if the area of activity-centric computing employed activity theory, at least partly.

The work on Activity Based Computing at Apple in the 1990s was influenced by Bødker's (1991), introduction of activity theory to HCI, as well as Norman's previous work employing some of the concepts developed in Russian sociocultural tradition (1991). In particular, this approach proposed an extended version of Leontiev's hierarchical model which was produced by adding the level of "tasks" (located between "activity" and "action") to the original three-level model (Leontiev, 1978, 1981).

The first version of the Kimura system (Voida et al., 2002) was developed without a reference to activity theory, but later the work adopted activity theory as a conceptual framework for both design and reflection (Voida et al., 2007). More recent explorations into activity-centric computing building on the work on Kimura system, such as design and evaluation of the Giornata system (Voida et al., 2008; Voida and Mynatt, 2009) are explicitly informed by activity theory.

The development of the UMEA system (Kaptelinin, 2003) and the range of technologies created within the Activity Based Computing project at the IT University of Copenhagen (e.g., Bardram, 2005; Bardram et al., 2006; Bardram, 2009) were, from the outset, inspired and guided by activity theory. In these cases technological designs were direct results of previous theoretical analyses and empirical studies of individual and collective activities, mediated by computer technologies.

In addition, we can discern a variety of indirect uses of activity theory in the area of activity-centric computing. These indirect uses include considering relevant concrete design solutions and technologies informed by activity theory (for instance, the systems, discussed above) without taking into account the theory itself, and employing the theory as the point of comparison when presenting and reflecting upon one's own approach.

An example of the latter is a systematic comparison of the Unified Activity Management framework and activity theory by Moran (2005a). Moran observes that while his work was not specifically inspired by activity theory, there are significant similarities between the frameworks: each proposes a conceptual apparatus for understanding and "parsing" what people do in their everyday life; each considers activities as hierarchically organized and inseparable from their objects; and each emphasizes the importance of understanding activities as developing over time. Moran also points to a number of differences between the frameworks. Unified Activity Management neither explicitly deals with motivation nor differentiates between conscious actions and routine operations, and is more directly concerned with formal process representations, interrelationships between activities, and shared representations.

In sum, while efforts such as the ROOMS system have not been related to activity theory, it would be fair to say that a substantial amount of work in activity-centric computing, especially in recent years, has been influenced by activity theory in one way or another.

CURRENT ISSUES AND PROSPECTS FOR FUTURE RESEARCH

Despite a sound rationale and relatively long history of exploration in HCI research, activity-centric computing is yet to become a widely accepted alternative to the currently dominant application-centric paradigm. Previous work on activity-centric computing is characterized by significant progress, but also reveals some issues that need to be addressed in future research. This section discusses some of these issues, as well as potential ways of addressing them (see also Bardram, 2005, for a related discussion).

A VARIETY OF PERSPECTIVES IN ACTIVITY-CENTRIC COMPUTING

The discussion in previous sections suggests that activity-centric computing is not a monolithic approach. Of course, there are basic features shared by all activity-centric systems. These features include integration of task-related resources (that is, cutting across different information hierarchies), making it possible for the user to easily and safely switch between activities (including stopping and resuming activities), and support for collaboration (for instance, facilitating user's communication with other participants of collaborative projects).

However, beyond this set of basic features lie substantial differences between concrete activity-centric technologies. One difference is between systems that offer personal/private vs. shared workspaces. While most systems discussed in this section (e.g., ROOMS, UMEA, Giornata) are personal, others such as Unified Activity Management and Bardram's Activity-based Computing, predominantly provide shared environments. Of course each approach serves legitimate needs, depending on the context.

The difference between personal and shared activity-centric systems has specific implications for their design, as well as how they are experienced by users. The most obvious distinction is related to privacy, which is necessarily rather limited in the case of shared workspaces. Even if a workspace does not record users' activities for legal purposes (see Bardram, 2005), it may still include some elements of monitoring the users and revealing to other participants the details of activities, which the users may not be willing to share. Less obvious but no less significant implications relate to tentative externalization, control, and activity representation.

Shared environments often make it difficult, and sometimes impossible, for a person to try out several alternatives by tentatively externalizing them and then choosing the best one. For instance, a personal computer user may apply different designs to a set of presentation slides to see which design looks best. In a shared environment, the user needs to "check out" an information object or in some way prevent the propagation of undesirable changes throughout the collective activity. This necessity may have the undesirable side effect of preventing spontaneous tentative externalization by individual users. Furthermore, collaborative activities supported by shared activity-centric environments may be characterized by a marked power difference among participants in which some participants have less control over the environment.

Finally, while shared activity-centric systems require that activities be explicitly represented, for personal systems it is not a necessary requirement (even though personal systems can include explicit representations, as well). An implicit representation of activities—e.g., describing a set of relevant resources without explicitly specifying the goals, sub-goals, deadlines, etc.—may be sufficient for a single user of a system. In case of shared activities it may need to be supplemented with an explicit representation (especially during a hand off, Bardram, (2005)) to ensure a common understanding of the structure and status of an activity by different participants.

The variety of activity-centric technologies that have emerged in HCI suggests that instead of creating an "ideal" activity-centric system, designers should aim at creating an activity-centric system which would be a good fit for a particular type of context, such as hospitals, corporate environments, personal computing, and so forth.

DESIGN CHALLENGES AND SOLUTIONS

Current work on activity-centric systems indicates that there are a number of remaining challenges to be addressed in the future.

Activity parsing

Integration of resources in activity-centric computing systems cuts across different types of information objects, but not different activities. An activity-centric system can only be useful if collections of resources, linked to their respective activities, are kept separate from one another. In order to ensure that information objects linked to different activities do not mix together, a system should be able to map resources and other information to specific activities.

The strategies employed in current activity-centric systems for differentiating between separate activities can be divided into three approaches: space-based, tag-based, and inference-based strategies.

Systems adopting the space-based approach such as ROOMS, the Task Gallery, and Giornata, provide multiple workspaces (e.g., virtual desktops), dedicated to particular activities or groups of activities. The user sets up a dedicated space as an activity context; everything taking place in the space is linked to the activity at hand, while information objects related to other activities are not displayed at all. Switching between spaces indicates to the system that the user is switching between different activities, which ensures that events and objects corresponding to the different activities are not mixed together.

Tag-based systems, such as UMEA or "project" labels in some versions of Mac OS, allow the user to simultaneously work with information objects belonging to different activities displayed in the same workspace. The objects are linked to their respective activities logically, but not necessarily spatially. Finally, inference-based systems such as TaskTracer employ various types of indirect evidence to make an informed guess about the resources the user might need to carry out the task at hand, and provide convenient access to the resources at appropriate points in time.

The main challenge for designing effective and efficient support for activity parsing is finding a trade-off between the potentially conflicting requirements of flexible integration, low overhead, and reliability. Space-based systems reliably keep different activities apart, but when the user needs to combine information objects from different activity contexts to carry out the task at hand, it may be difficult because of the strict separation between activity spaces. Tag-based systems allow for flexible organization of resources linked to different activities, but maintaining tags may create increased overhead. Inference-based systems may radically decrease activity management overhead but are inherently inaccurate, or "noisy"(Moran, 2005a) and therefore may not be reliable enough.

Relative strengths and weaknesses of different activity parsing strategies may depend on various factors. For instance, the advantages of space-based systems can only be enjoyed if large display surfaces, allowing the user to simultaneously view and manage several activity-specific workspaces, are provided[8]. Inference-based systems may be more reliable when different activities are associated with non-overlapping sets of resources compared to when the same resources are shared by several activities. Understanding advantages and disadvantages of different activity parsing strategies requires further research. An intriguing related issue is possible ways to combine several strategies within a single system. One such effort is the UMEA system, which allows the user to select one project from a list and then automatically adds project tags to all resources employed by the user, until the user switches to another project (or quits the system). The underlying strategy can be classified as predominantly tag-based but the system also employs some inference to minimize overhead.

Managing collections of diverse resources within an activity
Sets, or "packages," of diverse information objects, linked to an activity, should be presented to users in a consistent way to make it possible to view, organize, integrate, and otherwise manage a whole set of activity-related materials. Existing systems support such integration and coordination of an activity-specific work context by creating a configuration of open windows. However, such work contexts in traditional desktop systems are not

persistent and typically need to be restored when the person returns to the activity at hand after a break.

The work on activity-centric systems has explored a number of solutions that would allow the user to bundle diverse activity-related resources together and manage them as one unit. The main direction is to find appropriate ways to integrate abstract representations of information objects. Various abstract representations are commonly used in computing systems to manage collections of information objects, in particular, by providing overviews the collections. For instance, a document may be represented as a tile in the TaskBar, an icon in a folder window, or a file name on a "Recent documents" list. Such representations allow the user to get overviews of open windows, folder content, or recently edited text documents, and use the representation to select, open, delete, etc., the information objects. In traditional desktop systems such abstract representations are more difficult to integrate across different information hierarchies than open windows. The strategies for overcoming this limitation, proposed in the design of activity-centric systems, include grouping several TaskBar tiles together (GroupBar, Robertson et al., 2007), extending a representation of an information hierarchy, such as file system, by adding representations of relevant items from other hierarchies, such as web browser favorites (WorkSpaceMirror, Boardman and Sasse, 2004), and creating an integrated system of pointers that provides references to various types of information objects (e.g., lists of resources in UMEA or TaskTracer).

Managing collections of activities

People, both individuals and groups, are typically involved in several activities taking place generally in parallel (Barreau and Nardi, 1995; Cypher, 1986). Therefore, managing collections and not just isolated activities is one of the challenges for activity-centric systems. In current systems, the management of a collection is typically supported by providing various types of overviews of the user's activities and making it possible to switch between the overviews and contexts of particular activities. The most elaborated set of tools for presenting activities and their relationships is proposed within the Unified Activity Management project which reflects the special focus of the project on "meta-activities," that is activities directed at other activities. Most other activity-centric systems employ relatively simple representations of collections of activities, such as lists extended with some PIM features, e.g., deadlines.

EVALUATING ACTIVITY-CENTRIC TECHNOLOGIES AND ENVIRONMENTS

Most activity-centric systems have been evaluated in a variety of empirical studies including workshops and focus groups, brief usability testing sessions, small-scale trial implementations, and full-scale deployment in real-life contexts over extended periods of time (Balakrishnan et al., 2010; Bardram, 2007; Boardman and Sasse, 2004; Dragunov et al., 2005; Kaptelinin, 2003; Voida and Mynatt, 2009). The results of most of these studies suggest that such systems help users overcome fragmentation of their workspaces (Balakrishnan et al., 2010), support focus on the content of their work rather than technological issues (Bardram, 2007), and provide good user experience (Voida and Mynatt, 2009). For instance, users of the UMEA system appreciated the possibility to access various types of project-related resources "from within one place" (Kaptelinin, 2003), and users of the Giornata system mentioned that saving documents in project-specific workspaces "feels better than filing"(Voida and Mynatt, 2009).

Further studies are needed to properly assess specific advantages and disadvantages of activity-centric systems, as well as their underlying design approaches. For a couple reasons, interpretation of existing evaluation studies is somewhat problematic. First, activity-centric systems differ from one another. A key objective of the design of a system can be, for instance, integrating diverse resources around the activity at hand, supporting activity switching and its continuity across locations and technologies, promoting reflection and continuous development, or a combination thereof. These objectives are different for different systems, which makes it difficult to compare and generalize the results of the evaluation studies. Second, even though some of the studies analyzed long term user experiences with activity-centric systems, the time scope may still be insufficient, since both advantages and disadvantages of activity-centric systems can only become obvious when the systems are fully integrated into everyday practices of their users.

---

[8]The advantages do not necessarily scale up to wall-size displays, since such displays may incur additional costs; for instance, they may make it necessary for the user to move a few meters to switch between simultaneously displayed workspaces.

CHAPTER 6

Activity theory and the development of HCI

INTRODUCTION

As a final step toward generatively linking activity theory with current developments in HCI, we return to some of the concerns raised in Chapter 1, in particular the notion that purposeful collaborative transformation of the world finds expression in theory. We address recent research in human-computer interaction that could fruitfully deploy a theoretical approach such as activity theory. As a point of departure, as well as homage, we use the foundational human information processor model (Card et al., 1983) as a touchstone. We leverage the model for what it tells us about aspects of HCI historically and in the contemporary moment.

While HCI has changed in countless ways since 1983, the human information processor model retains significant influence (Clemmensen, 2006). It deserves our continuing admiration for establishing a solid basis for the scientific study of HCI. In the following analysis, the model stands as a contrastive point of reference for certain aspects of newer work which we will call "human needs HCI" or "hn-HCI." This work comprises a cluster of several ambitious streams of research that have emerged in the last five years. The research is historically grounded, shaped around complex real world problem spaces, and conceived as a response to these problems. hn-HCI foregrounds sociotechnical environments that speak to urgent human needs. This focus contrasts with "research projects and commercial undertakings focused . . . on perceived needs or manufactured needs" (Tomlinson et al., 2012). We use the term hn-HCI not to create dichotomous categories of HCI research, but to bring forward and celebrate research with clear commitments to social justice, equity, and goals beyond profit, or, as Stetsenko (2008) says (in her passionate way), "goals including the shift away from narrowly economic interests, unfair international policies, mindless consumption, and pernicious instrumentalism." hn-HCI research includes (but is not limited to) *sustainable HCI, interactive and collaborative technologies for development* (ICTD), *crisis informatics, comparative informatics*, and *collapse computing*. This research is not wholly contained within HCI, but HCI has made major contributions, helping shape agendas and introduce unique perspectives.

Projects in hn-HCI, and the trends to which they have given rise, contribute to what Clemmensen calls "a rush of different theories and frameworks into HCI" (2006) (some of which we have analyzed in past discussions of distributed cognition, situated action, and so on [Kaptelinin and Nardi, 2006; Nardi, 1996a]). How do we understand these trends and their needs for theories and frameworks? In this chapter we discuss hn-HCI and suggest how activity theory may prove useful in supporting its development. We appropriate the human information processor model—with its persistently influential intellectual commitments to controlled lab studies, a nomothetic, ahistorical approach, and the generalizability of "mechanisms" of action—in order to throw a light on the particularly difficult challenges hn-HCI has set for itself, and the conceptual needs that issue from those challenges. hn-HCI is not merely an instance of the computer reaching out to wider spheres of "users" (Grudin, 1990)—a standpoint in which the computer is still the center of the universe—but represents a bold turn toward conceiving HCI as an approach to design that analytically subordinates itself to concerns embedded in complex sociotechnical contexts. These contexts are characterized by aggravated, persistent problems—the environment, poverty, education, disasters, cross-cultural communication, societal decline.

While spanning a broad range of domains and topical areas, the research questions in each stream of hn-HCI share important characteristics: they are historically-sensitive; they presuppose analysis at the level of systems, and they are what we might loosely call "reality-based"[9]. Moving out of the lab and into the real world, hn-HCI research is motivated by deep interests in visible, sometimes shocking, problems of human life. The research is grounded in identifiable domains that provide the specific context of particular realities. hn-HCI presents a significant opportunity for studies of human-computer interaction to materially impact arenas of global concern. We locate activity theory as a framework that speaks to emergent problematics of hn-HCI.

Our discussion does not comprise a literature review of hn-HCI (which is beyond the scope of the book), but shows potential connections to activity theory. Research in hn-HCI has developed inductively, driven by heartfelt worries about resource scarcity, human rights, inequality, and other social anxieties, but also by perplexing problems of cross-cultural communication and collaboration in the workplace, as well as the impacts of ICTs on national and cultural identities. We believe that these inductively emergent areas of investigation should seek to mature into more conceptually sophisticated, theoretically informed practices. Not only would each individual stream of research benefit from firmer theoretical footing, but the individual streams should, over time, connect with one another, enriching, and mutually influencing one another. While the research streams may ultimately remain only loosely coalesced, it is important that theoretical and conceptual bridges encourage dialogue and cross-fertilization for greater impact. As Stetsenko (2008) noted, often the impact of sociocultural research is diminished as different schools of thought lodge themselves in separate academic domiciles, foreclosing opportunities for integration and greater influence.

We note that hn-HCI is a recent development. Publications have nearly all appeared since 2007. How is it that HCI has developed so powerfully so recently? It is difficult to say with certainty "why now," but we think that two causes are evident. First, HCI has matured into a robust sub-discipline of research lending scholars and practitioners confidence and assurance enough to tackle difficult problems of wide scope. Second, many in the community feel that global problems and issues seem only to intensify. Rather than moving toward solutions, the difficulties of our times measurably deepen (Diamond, 2004; Tainter, 1990, 2006; Vardi, 2009; see Tomlinson et al., 2012). hn-HCI is a response to a shared sense that HCI has, in the intervening years since the human information processor model grounded us in a rigorous science, developed sufficiently that we can and should do some good, taking action on troubling issues that are ever more plainly visible, and call for our attention.

hn-HCI

Perhaps the most dramatic instance of the power of hn-HCI to capture the imaginations and energies of researchers in our field is the meteoric rise of studies of *sustainable HCI* (Blevis, 2007; Blevis and Stolterman, 2007; Huang et al., 2009; Mankoff et al., 2008; Tomlinson, 2010). Sustainable HCI is concerned with: (1) designing technologies that reduce impacts on the environment (e.g., through longer cycles of obsolescence; see Blevis, 2007) and (2) designing technologies that help people reduce impact on the environment through behavioral change (such as digital meters informing people of their energy use, e.g., Amsel and Tomlinson, 2010; Mankoff et al., 2007). In an analysis of the literature in sustainable HCI, DiSalvo, Sengers and Brynjarsdóttir (2010a) report that heterogeneous methods, orientations, and approaches characterize what they call the "explosive growth" of sustainable HCI. The authors point to its near overnight success as a visible and valued focus of research in HCI. They observe that broad issues of culture, lifestyle, democracy, participation, politics, and professional design practice infuse discussions of sustainable HCI. This "explosion" of interest began in 2007, and marks a watershed as HCI takes on problems of significantly increased scope.

However, DiSalvo, Sengers, and Brynjarsdóttir (2010b) also observe that HCI may not be fully ready conceptually and methodologically to address the problems sustainable HCI seeks to solve.

[T]he packageable methods popular in HCI map poorly to sustainability because they fail to take into account the complexity of the problem (Blevis, 2007) . . . [D]esign driven by formal models of user needs leads to rapid obsolescence when new needs are found (Wakkary and Tanenbaum, 2009) . . . [E]valuation of long-term and systemic effects is a blind spot for HCI (Huang et al., 2009; Nathan, 2008).

We agree with this assessment. DiSalvo, Sengers, and Brynjarsdóttir situate sustainable HCI exactly within the context of the kinds of problems that must be analyzed, as we have argued, with historical sensitivity, attention to complex systems, and an eye to reality-based solutions. As Kuutti (2011) remarks, there are "not that many social theories" that encompass these perspectives. Activity theory is thus a leading candidate. In particular, activity theory emphasizes the centrality of artifacts—a theoretical position shared by only a few other theories such as actor-network theory (see Kaptelinin and Nardi, 2006). Historically, most social theories have ignored artifacts, or seen them as epiphenomenal, or conceived them as props for discourse, the maintenance of social order, or the fostering of interpersonal relations (see Huizing and Cavanagh, 2011).

Studies of ICTD set their sights on a constellation of issues as challenging as those of sustainable HCI. ICTD asks nothing less than that we move toward "making life better for the least privileged people of the world" (Toyama, 2010). Work in ICTD is concerned with improvements in technology and infrastructure for those living in chronically dire economic circumstances (Burrell, 2009; Le Dantec and Edwards, 2008; Patterson et al., 2009; Sambasivan et al., 2010; Woelfer et al., 2011).

The field of *crisis informatics* addresses saving lives and rebuilding infrastructure in the context of consequential events including natural disasters and political disruptions (Al-Ani et al., 2012; Mark et al., 2012; Palen et al., 2007; Qu et al., 2009; Shlovski et al., 2010; Starbird and Palen, 2011; Torrey et al., 2007). *Collapse computing* (Tomlinson et al., 2012; Wong, 2009, see Diamond, 2004; Tainter, 1990, 2006; Vardi, 2009) picks up where local disasters leave off, addressing the possibility of persistent, pervasive societal decay. Collapse computing is grounded in the orienting observation that

Research in many fields argues that contemporary global industrial civilization will not persist in its current form, and may, like many past human societies, eventually collapse. Arguments in environmental studies, anthropology, and other fields indicate that this transformation could begin within the next half-century. While imminent collapse is far from certain, it is prudent to consider now how to develop sociotechnical systems for use in these scenarios (Tomlinson et al., 2012).

Collapse computing is thus a preemptive strike to anticipate the kinds of ICT solutions collapse might entail, drawing on work in sustainable HCI, ICTD, and crisis informatics, but going well beyond in predicting a more seriously dysfunctional future. Collapse computing entertains the premise of a vivid if disturbing historical parable that recounts the rise and fall of most complex societies. Collapse computing's narrative continues, more hopefully, to indicate "the potential contribution that the field of HCI can make to the eventuality of collapse" (Tomlinson et al., 2012).

Somewhat less urgently, but still crucially important, is the study of comparative informatics which seeks to make visible, in our global world, both difference and similarity, in subtle ways that can influence design (Nardi et al., 2011). Comparative informatics

systematically examines similarities and differences in the ICT life cycle—design, development, deployment, adoption, use, impact, and evaluation—in contexts including cultures, regions, nations, generations, socioeconomic classes, gender, organizations, and technologies. The objective is to generate nuanced, critical understandings of technology in human life in the world we inhabit together (p. 1).

As an example, the authors describe how study of the "white rat" of HCI—word processing—does not necessarily encompass the universal set of technologies and results we might suppose. Subtle technological differences decenter national identity; for example the Danish vowels æ, ø, and å are not always available on standard keyboards and smartphones (see also Clemmensen 2010). Danish users must get along without these vowels, or use sequences of control keys to type them. Yet these letters represent core sounds in Danish, and were institutionally systematized into the language decades ago in the official Retskrivningsordbog udgivet af Dansk Sprognævn (1955). Clemmensen (2010) notes also that "not before the year 2003 were Danish letters allowed in domain names, which for the first time allowed Danish companies like Carlsberg to spell beer on websites in the correct way: 'øl'." As HCI scholars and practitioners, we must ask how such history and cultural identity bear on our practice of design, and how we may conceive diversity in ways that go beyond superficial "localization." New formulations are imperative as concerns regarding national character and personhood may be at stake.

The original human information processor model argued for the importance of examining diversity in user populations and tasks of interest. As Clemmensen (2006) observed,

In the [human information processor] framework, systems were designed for different task domains and task models. User interfaces of computers varied in dialogue style, input devices and display layout, and the human users had different intellectual abilities, computer experience, task knowledge, computer knowledge, cognitive style and perceptual-motor skills.

We find significant value in this argument. But at the same time, in a "hard science" gambit, the human information processor model rejected the historical, reality-based empirics necessary for hn-HCI. An ahistorical perspective continues to pervade HCI. Clemmensen (2006) discusses how it was argued that

The hard science psychology should focus on the use of theories that identified underlying mechanisms as opposed to an insufficient soft science HCI psychology consisting of ". . . the judgment of the theorists, the experience of the practitioners, the assessments of the users, or even the empirical evaluation of systems . . ." (Newell and Card, 1986)

It is remarkable that this conceptualization eschewed user experience and evaluation in favor of "mechanisms," and clearly it built no bridges to the study of what is necessary for the research entailed in hn-HCI. It is difficult to imagine a "hard science" orientation addressing, say, the role of digital technology in the stabilization of cultural identity, the use of technologies in the aftermath of a hurricane, or how we might conceive information technologies in the event of widespread political unrest or global declines in energy availability. hn-HCI must orient toward developing contingent, open-ended analyses that do not rest on "atomistic tasks" (see Carroll and Campbell, 1986) disconnected from historical context. As Clemmensen observed, the very nature of HCI systems in the human information processor model was defined at too low a level to scale to important problems of human-computer interaction (2006). hn-HCI, and its current popularity and rapid rise to prominence, indicate that firmer, deeper theoretical development is essential.

TIME, SPACE, SCOPE

The complexity inherent in hn-HCI gives rise to challenging analytics of time, space, and scope. While "context" is often invoked as what is missing in HCI research, we want to be more specific. We begin with time in discussing these problematics and their conceptual, methodological, and epistemological orientations.

HCI has long taken a cue from the human information processor model in accepting the imaginary of the timeless moment of the laboratory experiment. This moment reifies context-free generic tasks as its subject matter. In hn-HCI, tasks that putatively persist unchanged over time are replaced by the temporal dynamics of complex lived experiences occurring within powerful historical events and activities. The beginning of a disaster is different than its later stages. An impoverished school system that receives new computers is not the same school system that eventually negotiates its way toward more effective use of the technology. Design practices that at one time seemed benign are shown to set in motion deleterious environmental effects. Events and activities unfold within systems such as school systems, emergency response infrastructure, NGOs, governments, corporations. Clemmensen observed that underlying the human information processor model was a belief that it would be possible to conduct detailed studies of a set of "generic tasks" that would yield generalizable understandings across many domains (2006).

But as Kuutti (2011) counters,

> [M]ost theory suggestions have assumed the timeless, general, and abstract natural science model of theory. [T]he subject matter of design is of a historical nature, so a timeless theory is incapable of grasping the essentials of the field.

Kuutti argues that activity theory, which has been oriented toward history and development since its inception, is a "dynamically oriented alternative" theory for studies of human computer interaction. We concur, and further suggest that activity theory is especially pertinent to hn-HCI with its particular concerns arising directly out of specific historical events and conditions. Activity theory presupposes and theorizes change, rather than aiming at nomothetic generalization that more or less stops time.

An argument against the timeless moment of the laboratory is not an argument against experimentation, but opposes experimentation in which a roster of tasks is examined in laboratories under the assumption that experimental control is possible because (in part) the tasks are timeless. hn-HCI begins with an understanding of a mutable historical reality from which experiments may be devised, rather than the axiomatic belief that a tractable set of generic tasks exists that we can study in pure form. As discussed in Chapter 2, formative experiments emphasizing transformation over time are a key method in activity theory.

Kuutti observed that the acceptance of dynamism leads directly to a "sensitivity to history." All activities are historically formed, and they thus "carry with them the history of their development" (2011). A historical analysis of the development of an activity is a means by which to clarify and understand the current situation (Kuutti, 2011). Technology itself is always changing, intertwining with, and giving rise to changes in practice (Huizing and Cavanagh, 2011).

Stetsenko (2008) observes that "necessary components of a commitment to social transformation presuppose understanding that social institutions are malleable, historically contingent, and fluid, and therefore require a historically based understanding." By its very nature, hn-HCI embodies this stance. But its theoretical development is nascent; work to date has focused on consideration of technology within the compelling domains the work addresses rather than theoretical analysis or development.

We believe that activity theory's understandings of history and change are useful resources for the transformative project of hn-HCI. In particular, the emphasis on artifact mediation as a process of change is crucial. As Kuutti (2011) notes, "A typical way of inducing a purposeful change in an activity is re-mediation: change in some of the mediating artifacts." How do artifacts and their uses change, and what effects do the changes have? These considerations rarely arise in lab studies of the human information processor variety, or even field studies, yet they are crucial in the real world. Activity theory's emphasis on artifacts as mediators of change is central to the concerns of hn-HCI (see also Bødker and Andersen, 2005; Bødker and Klokmose, 2011).

Just as time is often deleted in our analyses, so is space. Cartesian space is important but we call special attention to human culture and identity as they emergently change across space. (Cartesian space itself is of course implicated in constructing and defending culture and identity.) ICTD and comparative informatics in particular investigate implicit assumptions about culture and identity that constitute universalizing moves to generalize. These moves often turn out to call on typified experience extracted and decontextualized from the geographical point of origin of a technology. For example, as word processing technology traveled from its original home in California the locale that established its typification—it carried with it presumptions of American usage. Eventually the design bumped up against other realities such as the Danish alphabet. These confrontations forced reexamination, but not before leading Danes to experiment with some awkward adaptations. For example, a Danish travel blog writer recounted how when using "un-Danish" computers, it was possible to write æ, ø and å with the following codes

æ : 0230

Æ : 0198

@ : 064

ø : 0248

Ø : 0216

å : 0229

Å : 0197

by holding down the alt key while typing the numeric code for each letter (Nardi, Clemmensen, and Vatrapu 2011). Clemmensen (2010) reported the exasperation of Danish domain name owners when the full Danish alphabet was finally accommodated in domain names:

I own a company "Åberg El," and we have through the past five years had our website on the following domains:

aaberg-el.com

aaberg-el.dk

aaberg-el.se

aaberg-el.no

These pages are well-known and constantly used by our customers. ÆØÅ is introduced as domain names, and suddenly Åberg-el must invest in the domains: åberg-el.com, etc . . . If you do not own both the domain with "aa" and that with "å," you risk losing either the old customers or potential customers. Even worse, a domain shark or a competitor bought the domain with either "aa" or "å" (Wenix, 2003, cited in Clemmensen).

As we traverse global space, encountering new cultures, practices, and identities, it is necessary that we acknowledge and theorize them, recognizing the unevenness of technological experience as it varies across space. Patterson et al. (2009) discussed the perils of "design at a distance," recounting how their design ideas formulated in the US were discarded one by one as they encountered reality in the actual cultural and geographical spaces of low-income Zambia and South Africa. The authors emphasized that identifying the particularities of specific spaces is essential and difficult:

[We believed] that we were one type of user, and Africans were a homogenous "other" kind of user. This was our implicit justification for doing initial background investigations with people from places as varied as Sierra Leone and Kenya, even though these were not the environments in which we were planning to deploy our technologies.

Finally, hn-HCI demands that we alter the usual scope of our analyses. Small laboratory studies, localized ethnographies, and the study of microinteractions in ethnomethodological investigations usually fail to get at what information philosopher Jannis Kallinikos (2004) memorably calls "essential strips of reality." Kallinikos argued that construals of technology "cannot be exhausted at the very interface upon which humans encounter technology. Essential strips of reality are not observable or even describable at the level of contextual encounters." Kallinikos points out that when sticking only to localized analyses, we misapprehend contemporary technologies and technological systems whose form and function (Kallinikos, 2012) go far beyond the user interface or simple notions of user experience. Large information systems implicated in our daily lives (banking systems, electronic patient record systems, databases of all kinds, for example) are outside the scope of traditional usability HCI metrics. Rather than being "adaptable," "customizable," or amenable to "interpretive flexibility," on the contrary, these systems exhibit considerable rigidity, usually making it impossible for users to fix errors (e.g., banking errors or misinformation about one's medical status or criminal history) without engaging large and sometimes daunting institutions. Rather than adhering to HCI's optimistic notions of user control, choice, and preference, these systems often entail serious risks such as wrongful caching and propagation of consequential information. The "user interface" is in fact a very small aspect of our experience with crucial everyday information systems.

Of course in traditional HCI this did not matter; the user interface was established as the key point of inquiry—the correct "strip of reality" to which our attentions were properly directed. But without quite realizing it, hn-HCI has, in its bottom-up, inductive way, relinquished narrowly conceived notions of user interaction, moving attention forward to issues of considerably larger scope. For example, Blevis (2007), in an award-winning CHI paper, indicates the need to reconstitute HCI so that we take seriously the entire life cycle of a technology, interpolating recycling, reuse, disposal, and so on, within focal HCI concerns. Palen et al. (2007) detail the intricacies of citizen-government relations in managing and responding to disasters, and what those societal-scale relations mean for HCI. Wong (2009) discusses the need to broaden the scope of HCI if research is to achieve meaningful results: "Researchers should . . . consider . . . the design context to be a world radically altered by environmental damage; solutions that fit into today's lifestyles risk irrelevance" (2009). Wong succinctly captures essential hn-HCI analytics: time (changing environmental damage), cultural space (certain lifestyles), and scope (the world). These analytics are not standalone "variables;" they represent mutually influencing, holistic conditions we must apprehend, and respond to, if our work is to avoid "risking irrelevance."

Within a larger context of human-centered computing, Kaptelinin and Bannon (2012) frame the argument by observing that HCI is still typically circumscribed by notions of technological products, but that we must appreciate more broadly construed "habitats." Kuutti (2010) notes that in Europe "user experience" research is badly undertheorized; there has even been a retreat to "personal, practice-grounded opinions" that "define what user experience means."

Throughout the years we have seen a steady stream of calls for more expansive, principled formulations to enlarge the scope of HCI beyond parochial limits of technological products and practice-oriented strategies (e.g., Bannon, 2011; Carmien et al., 2005; Fischer et al., 2004; Forlizzi, 2008; Friedman et al., 2006; Kirsh, 2001; Nardi, 1996a; Spinuzzi, 2003).

Bannon is clear that we have not yet achieved the potential of these approaches:

We should not believe that applying new labels such as "human centered" to HCI or computing or design in itself changes anything. Rather, the name change points to a more bottom-up process of rediscovering our human potential and reconstructing the very foundations on which we attempt to build any form of human-centered informatics (Bannon, 2011).

We suggest that while the development of broader conceptual and theoretical approaches has not been without impact in the field, Bannon is largely right about the urgent need for foundational work and more effective efforts. We hope that the considerable passion behind hn-HCI will be a catalyst that moves the field forward in ways it has not moved before. The powerful empirical realities of ICTD, collapse computing, and all of hn-HCI, constitute compelling strips of reality around which we can rally and organize as we move to "reconstruct the foundations" of HCI.

Ethical issues should be paramount in this reconstruction. Bannon (2011) notes that ethical inquiry often eludes us, advocating that as we "reimagine HCI," we must at the same time "act out" a better world. This proposition is exactly what drives hn-HCI. We are thus due for a major reappraisal of the scope and nature of research within the field of human-computer interaction.

ACTIVITY THEORY AND hn-HCI

Although activity theory is a psychological theory, as we saw in Chapter 2, from activity theory's earliest beginnings, human culture, history, and development were pillars of analysis. Activity theory has thus come to be known as cultural-historical activity theory. Miettinen et al. (2009) observe that activity theory is "a well-developed model of the structure and developmental dynamics of human activity, as well as a non-individualist theory of learning based on the concept of cultural mediation." The embodied, individual human person does not disappear in activity theory (as in approaches such as actor-network theory); rather, this person is defined—through the principles of mediation, development, and internalization-externalization—indivisibly in relation to culture and other people. Miettinen et al. (2009) emphasize Leontiev's (1978) axiom that consciousness and meaning are always formed in joint, collective activity. If one takes away nothing from activity theory but a disposition to examine history and culture in a principled way, the value of activity theory is assured.

However, it is not so easy to do even this much. Perhaps the difficulties of deeper analysis explain why we do not more readily engage history and culture in our research. Each presents its own problems of argumentation, rhetorical strategy, and epistemology. Added complexity does not always slot comfortably into ever shorter cycles of production that seem to characterize contemporary work patterns. As the world rushes past faster and faster (due in part to the very digital technologies we champion), the quiet and time needed to thoughtfully engage complex problems give way to quicker, dirtier solutions. Many current conference papers, for example, scarcely cite work more than ten years old, no matter how relevant it may be, much less dig deeply into the culture and history of the subject matter. When value is measured in number of publications and conference presentations, we experience insistent pressure to devise ways to carve up our research into the greatest number of "minimal meaningful units" to maximize measured value. It is perhaps no accident that activity theory originated in a profoundly different cultural era, one which we can hardly imagine today.

The world may press on us, but that does not negate that hn-HCI (and serious proposals for human-centered computing) demand the incorporation of exactly the cultural and historical elements activity theory established as essential. A position statement of the European Society for Socially Embedded Technologies (EUSSET, 2009) asks:

How can we respond to the inescapable "permanent tension" between the need for global systems and the enduring or emerging local concerns and issues, how can we design in support of cultural diversity, social inclusion, as well as social and environmental sustainability; how can we design for new forms of engagement and participation?

In taking these questions to heart, the principle of development in activity theory is a critical resource. A recursive concept, development can turn theory back on itself, prescribing that all theories—activity theory included—develop and respond to changing cultural and historical conditions. The "new forms of thinking about the human-technology relationship" that Bannon (2011) argues for will arise when we push ourselves theoretically.

As an example, such development of activity theory is evident in Bødker and Andersen's (2005) proposal for analysis of "complex mediation" in sociotechnical systems. Complex mediation comprises two parts: "multi-mediation" in which multiple technologies and their interrelations form the backbone of empirical/theoretical analysis, and semiotic analysis.

The authors take a core concept from activity theory—mediation—and develop it into a more nuanced, yet practical notion of multi-mediation, noting that while most HCI analyses concern a single technological mediator, in reality, activities generally entail multiple mediators in varying configurations. Bødker and Andersen identify key configurations as (1) co-occurring mediators, (2) mediators at different levels, and (3) chains of mediators. They argue that we should design for multiple mediators rather than "singular use."

The authors weave semiotic analysis into the scheme to draw attention to both instrumental and semiotic activities. While Vygotsky (1962, 1978) was deeply involved with semiotics, semiotic concerns faded to some degree in later treatments of activity theory. Bødker and Andersen point to this as a lack, and develop careful argumentation accentuating that instrumentality and semiosis are necessarily bound up with one another, and that we need to develop analytics to contain both.

Complex mediation maps nicely to instances of hn-HCI; for example, Blevis's call for sustainable product design ideas such as Nelson and Stolterman's (2003) "ensoulment." Ensoulment—an emotional disposition of a customer toward a product—favors designs with long term appeal over those presuming more immediate obsolescence. Strategies such as ensoulment constitute a semiotic move—they enhance the scope of HCI's typical concerns beyond, for example, the instrumentalities of usability.

The enormity of this larger semiotic task within hn-HCI is evident in an anecdote from Patterson et al. (2009) who recount an event in their research on mobile phones in Africa:

One of our Zambian hosts even referred to a class of cell phones as "disposable;" he would buy one of these when traveling to a different region, to maximize connectivity and minimize cost, and then discard the phone upon return.

Even in less economically secure regions, a pervasive acceptance of disposability as a rational strategy shapes action. This small anecdote is a world in a grain of sand in illustrating the challenges of hn-HCI. The ethical issues to which Bannon points infuse this story; the authors lack a clear moral directive regarding how to confront practice in other cultures that contradicts our own hoped for values (such as sustainability). The sheer hugeness of the problem of finding out what it is that people are doing and what their actions mean to them presents a formidable challenge in attaining cogent semiotic understanding.

Patterson et al. (2009) also reported the need to design with assemblages of multiple mediators in mind. In their research, phone cards, Wi-Fi antennas, electrical adapters, and software applications were necessary, as well as mobile phones themselves. The authors present this finding as an "aha" moment discovered through intensive field research— and as a big surprise.

We argue that with a less ad hoc approach, a more theoretically ambitious reckoning, the authors might have used activity theory, perhaps Bødker and Andersen's understandings of multiple mediators, to prepare themselves to anticipate the complexity they encountered. Details could well remain obscure until arrival in the field, but more nuanced preparation and envisagement would be possible. As the old saying goes, there is nothing so practical as a good theory.

CONCLUSION

Stetsenko (2008) remarks that scholars moving toward more intense study of their domains often begin to reinvent the basics of activity theory as they seek to ground the work conceptually. We hope, with this book, to save you the trouble! It has been our intent to gather together activity theory basics in the most straightforward way possible, summarizing nearly 100 years of work that has traveled slowly but steadily from its beginnings in Soviet

Russia, into Europe, North America, and Asia. We close the book with tremendous optimism. In this chapter we identified and characterized hn-HCI, a promising development in studies of human-computer interaction. We believe activity theory can enhance this line of research. We are inspired to see HCI scholarship that puts problems first, leaving a crucial opening for theory. We discussed the close match between the concerns of hn-HCI and core activity theory precepts: history, culture, development, technological mediation. We see these notions sneaking into hn-HCI studies, but in tentative, piecemeal ways. This book should enable readers to appropriate the concepts in a more integrated, principled manner.

Perhaps most importantly, we invite readers to visit the work of the activity theory scholars whose research we have discussed. The proof of the pudding ultimately lies in the thoughtful contributions of these members of the HCI community (and beyond). The research practices in this work tell a tale of their own: multi-year projects, intensive participant-observation, participatory design, theoretical reflection and development, and dedication to understanding culture and history. These practices are not just common sense; they arise directly from the theoretical concerns of activity theory and its characterization of human activity. The payoff of careful, patient inquiry lies in attaining knowledge derived from the application of a theory that insists that what is important in human life cannot always be seen in few moments, that we possess a strong potential for human development, and that culture and history are shaping but not determinative forces.

We return to Stetsenko's cautionary words on the profound costs of ignoring theory. hn-HCI in particular, but HCI at large as well, represent a significant progressive project within the larger field of computer science. The human face of computing is vivid and present because of the labors of the HCI community. To push our concerns forward, we can grow HCI with a theory as powerful and encompassing as the reductionist theories we discussed as we opened the book. Activity theory's message, in place of a story of immutable genetics, is that culture and history matter, that change belongs to us, that a move to a "collaborative historical becoming," as Stetsenko says, is a challenge we can and should embrace. The reductionist synthesis prevails because it is unafraid to ask what it means to be human, and to offer a definite (if simplistic, in our view) answer. Absent other answers, the confident, crisply stated propositions issuing from the neuro-sociobiological camp reach wider publics, and come to constitute the only voice in the conversation. It is an irony of the doctrine of polyvocality that when we listen to many voices, each saying its own thing, we hear the unintelligible, amounting to a silence.

One answer to this silence is a more collaborative, focused conversation about theory. Collaborative transformation of the world is an ongoing, seemingly unstoppable human activity. Stepping into the stream of historical change, we can contribute to that change through grounded, reflective action informed by the articulation of coherent theory.

[9]In using the term reality-based, we reference broad historical realities, not user interface techniques based on nondigital understandings, e.g., naive physics (see Jacob et al., 2008).

Bibliography

Activity-based computing (n.d.) `http://activitybasedcomputing.org/` Cited on page(s) 59

Al-Ani, B., Mark, G., Chung, J., and Jones, J. (2012) The Egyptian blogosphere during the revolution: A narrative of counter-power. *Proc. CSCW 2012*. NY: ACM. DOI: 10.1145/2145204.2145213 Cited on page(s) 68

Albrechtsen, H., Andersen, H., Bødker, S., and Pejtersen. A. (2001) Affordances in activity theory and cognitive systems engineering. Risø-R-1287 (EN). Roskilde: Risø National Laboratory. `http://130.226.56.153/rispubl/SYS/syspdf/ris-r-1287.pdf` Cited on page(s) 5

Amsel, N. and Tomlinson, B. (2010) Green tracker: A tool for estimating the energy consumption of software. *Proc. CHI 2010*. NY: ACM. Pp. 3337–3342. DOI: 10.1145/1753846.1753981 Cited on page(s) 67

Aricvitch, I. and van der Veer, R. (1995) Furthering the internalization debate: Gal'perin's contribution. *Human Development* 38: 113–126. Cited on page(s) 18

Baerentsen, K. and Trettvik, J. (2002) An activity theory approach to affordance. *Proc. NordiCHI 2002*. NY: ACM. Pp. 51–60. DOI: 10.1145/572020.572028 Cited on page(s) 5

Balakrishnan, A. D., Matthews, T., and Moran, T. P. (2010) Fitting an activity-centric system into an ecology of workplace tools. *Proc. CHI 2010*. NY: ACM. Pp. 787–790. DOI: 10.1145/1753326.1753441 Cited on page(s) 58, 64

Bannon, L., Cypher, A., Greenspan, S., Monty, M. L. (1983) Evaluation and analysis of users' activity organization. *Proc. CHI 1983*. NY: ACM. Pp. 54–57. Cited on page(s) 56

Bannon, L. (1991) From human factors to human actors: The role of psychology and human-computer interaction studies in system design. In J. Greenbaum and M. Kyng (eds.), *Design at Work: Cooperative Design of Computer Systems*. Hillsdale, N.J.: Lawrence Erlbaum. Pp. 25–44. Cited on page(s) 1, 6

Bannon, L. (2011) Reimagining HCI: Toward a more human-centered perspective. *Interactions* 18 (4): 50–57. DOI: 10.1145/1978822.1978833 Cited on page(s) 73, 74

Bardram, J. (2005) Activity-based computing: Support for mobility and collaboration in ubiquitous computing. *Pers. Ubiquit. Comput.* 9: 312–322. DOI: 10.1007/s00779-004-0335-2 Cited on page(s) 58, 59, 60, 61

Bardram, J., Bunde-Pedersen, J., and Soegaard, M. (2006) Support for activity-based computing in a personal computing operating system. *Proc. CHI 2006*. NY: ACM. DOI: 10.1145/1124772.1124805 Cited on page(s) 55, 58, 60

Bardram, J. (2007) From desktop task management to ubiquitous activity-based computing. In V. Kaptelinin and M. Czerwinski (eds.), *Beyond the desktop metaphor: Creating integrated digital work environments*. MIT Press. Pp. 223–259. Cited on page(s) 58, 64

Bardram, J. (2009) Activity-based computing for medical work in hospitals. *ACM TOCHI* 16(2): 1–36. DOI: 10.1145/1534903.1534907 Cited on page(s) 58, 59, 60

Bargas-Avila, J. and Hornbaeck, K. (2011) Old wine in new bottles or novel challenges: A critical analysis of empirical studies of user experience. *Proc. CHI 2011*. NY: ACM. Pp. 2689–2698. DOI: 10.1145/1978942.1979336 Cited on page(s) 47

Barreau, D. and Nardi, B. (1995) Finding and reminding: File organization from the desktop. *SIGCHI Bulletin* 27: 39–43. DOI: 10.1145/221296.221307 Cited on page(s) 63

Basov, M. Ia. (1991) The organization of processes of behavior (a structural analysis) (originally published in Russian in 1931). *Journal of Russian and East European Psychology* 29(5): 14–83. DOI: 10.2753/RPO1061-0405290514 Cited on page(s) 14

Baumer, E. and Tomlinson, B. (2011) Comparing activity theory with distributed cognition for video analysis: Beyond "kicking the tires." *Proc. CHI 2011*. NY: ACM. DOI: 10.1145/1978942.1978962 Cited on page(s) 51

Bedny, G. Z. and Harris, S. R. (2005) The systemic-structural theory of activity: Applications to the study of human work. *Mind, Culture and Activity* 12(2): 90–112. Cited on page(s) 36

Bellotti, V., Ducheneaut, N., Howard, M., and Smith, J. (2003). Taking email to task: The design and evaluation of a task management centered email tool. *Proc. CHI 2003*. NY: ACM. DOI: 10.1145/642611.642672 Cited on page(s) 57

Bertelsen, O. and Bødker, S. (2003) Activity theory. In J. Carroll (ed.), *HCI Models, Theories, and Frameworks: Toward a Multidisciplinary Science*. Amsterdam: Morgan Kaufmann. Pp. 291–324. Cited on page(s) 5

Blevis, E. (2007) Sustainable interaction design: Invention & disposal, renewal & reuse. *Proc. CHI 2007.* NY: ACM. Pp. 503–512. DOI: 10.1145/1240624.1240705 Cited on page(s) 67, 72

Blevis, E. and Stolterman, E. (2007) Ensoulment and sustainable interaction design. *Proceedings of the International Association of Design Research Societies Conference IASDR 2007.* HKPT. Cited on page(s) 67

Boardman, R. and Sasse, M. A. (2004) "Stuff goes into the computer and doesn't come out:" A cross-tool study of personal information management. *Proc. CHI 2004.* NY: ACM. Pp. 583–590. DOI: 10.1145/985692.985766 Cited on page(s) 55, 57, 63, 64

Bødker, S. (1989) A human activity approach to user interfaces. *Human Computer Interaction* 4: 171–195. DOI: 10.1207/s15327051hci0403_1 Cited on page(s) 5, 11

Bødker, S. (1991) *Through the interface: A human activity approach to user interface design.* Hillsdale, NJ: Lawrence Erlbaum. Cited on page(s) 1, 5, 6, 30, 46, 59

Bødker, S. and Andersen, P. B. (2005) Complex mediation. *Human Computer Interaction* 20: 353–402. DOI: 10.1207/s15327051hci2004_1 Cited on page(s) 5, 71, 74

Bødker, S. and Klokmose, N. (2011) The Human-Artifact Model: An activity theoretical approach to artifact ecologies. *Human Computer Interaction* 26: 315–371. Cited on page(s) 8, 71

Brentano, F. (1987) On the existence of God: Lectures given at the universities of Wurzburg and Vienna, 1868–1891. In S. Krantz (ed.), *Nijhoff International Philosophy Series,* Vol. 29. Zoetermeer: Martinus Nijhoff International. Cited on page(s) 51

Brushlinsky, A. and Aboulhanova-Slavskaya, K. (2000) The historical context and modern denotations of the fundamental work by S. L. Rubinshtein. *Afterword to the 4th edition of Foundations of General Psychology* (in Russian). St. Petersburg, Russia: Piter. Cited on page(s) 14

Bryant, S. L., Forte, A., and Bruckman, A. (2005) Becoming Wikipedian: Transformation of participation in a collaborative online encyclopedia. *Proc. GROUP 2005.* NY: ACM. DOI: 10.1145/1099203.1099205 Cited on page(s) 8

Buchenau, M. and Suri, J. (2000) Experience prototyping. *Proc. DIS'2000.* NY: ACM. Pp. 424–433. DOI: 10.1145/347642.347802 Cited on page(s) 47

Burrell, J. (2009) What constitutes good ICTD research? *Information Technologies and International Development* 5(3): 82–94. Cited on page(s) 68

Callon, M. (1986) Some elements of a sociology of translations: Domestication of the scallops and the fishermen of St. Brieuc Bay. In J. Law (ed.), *Power, Action and Belief*. London: Routledge and Kegan Paul. Pp. 196–233. Cited on page(s) 50

Card, S., Moran, T. P. and Newell, A. (1983) *The Psychology of Human-Computer Interaction*. Hillsdale, NJ: Lawrence Erlbaum. Cited on page(s) 1, 65

Card, S. and Henderson, A. (1987) A multiple virtual-workspace interface to support user task switching. *Proc. CHI 87*. NY: ACM. DOI: 10.1145/30851.30860 Cited on page(s) 56

Carmien, S., Dawe, M., Fischer, G., Gorman, A., Kintsch, A., and Sullivan, J. (2005) Socio-technical environments supporting people with cognitive disabilities using public transportation. *ACM TOCHI* 12: 233–262. DOI: 10.1145/1067860.1067865 Cited on page(s) 73

Carroll, J. and Campbell, R. (1986) Softening up hard science: Reply to Newell and Card. *Human Computer Interaction* 2: 227–49. Cited on page(s) 69

Carroll, J. (ed.), (1991) *Designing Interaction: Psychology at the Human-Computer Interface*. Cambridge: Cambridge University Press. Cited on page(s) 1, 32

Carroll, J.M., Rosson, M.B., Convertino, G., and Ganoe, C. (2006) Awareness and teamwork in computer-supported collaborations. *Interacting with Computers* 18: 21–46. DOI: 10.1016/j.intcom.2005.05.005 Cited on page(s) 8

Carroll, J.M. (2011) Human Computer Interaction (HCI). In M. Soegaard and R. F. Dam (eds.), *Encyclopedia of Human-Computer Interaction*. Available online at http://www.interaction-design.org/encyclopedia/human_computer_interaction_hci.html Cited on page(s) 2

Carroll, J.M. (2012) Commentary on 'Activity Theory' by Victor Kaptelinin. Retrieved 15 March 2012 from Interaction-Design.org: http://www.interaction-design.org/encyclopedia/activity_theory.html#john+m.+carroll Cited on page(s) 8

Christensen, H. and Bardram, J. (2002) Supporting human activities — exploring activity-centered computing. *Proc. UbiComp 2002*. (Lecture Notes in Computer Science 2498). Berlin: Springer. Pp. 107–116. DOI: 10.1007/3-540-45809-3_8 Cited on page(s) 58

Clemmensen, T. (2006) Whatever happened to the psychology of human-computer interaction? *Information Technology & People* 19(2): 121–151. Cited on page(s) 65

Clemmensen, T. (2010) Regional styles of human-computer interaction. *Proceedings of the 3rd international conference on Intercultural collaboration*. Pp. 219–222. ACM, Copenhagen, Denmark. Cited on page(s) 68, 69

Cole, M. and Engeström, Y. (1993) A cultural-historical approach to distributed cognition. In G. Salomon (ed.), *Distributed Cognitions: Psychological and Educational Considerations*. New York: Cambridge University Press. Pp. 1–46. Cited on page(s) 32

Cole, M. (1996) *Cultural Psychology: A Once and Future Discipline*. Cambridge: The Belknap Press of Harvard University Press. Cited on page(s) 46

Cooper, G. and Bowers, J. (1995) Representing the user: Notes on the disciplinary rhetoric of human-computer interaction. In P. Thomas (ed.), *The Social and Interactional Dimensions of Human-Computer Interfaces*. New York: Cambridge University Press. Pp. 48–66. Cited on page(s) 1

CRADLE, Center for Research on Activity, Development and Learning (n.d.). http://www.helsinki.fi/cradle/index.htm Cited on page(s) 35, 46

Cypher, A. (1986) The structure of users' activities. In D. Norman and S. Draper (eds.), *User Centered System Design, New Perspectives on Human-Computer Interaction*. Hillsdale, NJ: Lawrence Erlbaum. Pp. 243–264. Cited on page(s) 56, 63

Diamond, J. (2004) *Collapse: How Societies Choose to Fail or Succeed*. Viking Adult. Cited on page(s) 67, 68

DiSalvo, C., Sengers, P., and Brynjarsdóttir, H. (2010a) Mapping the landscape of sustainable HCI. *Proc. CHI 2010*. NY: ACM. Pp. 1975–1984. DOI: 10.1145/1753326.1753625 Cited on page(s) 67

DiSalvo, C., Sengers, P., and Brynjarsdóttir, H. (2010b) Navigating the terrain of sustainable HCI. *Interactions* 17: 22–25. Cited on page(s) 67

Dourish, P. (2001) *Where the Action Is: The Foundations of Embodied Interaction*. Cambridge: MIT Press. Cited on page(s) 29, 50, 51, 52

Dragunov, A., Dietterich, T. G., Johnsrude, K., McLaughlin, M., Li, L., and Herlocker, J. L. (2005) TaskTracer: A desktop environment to support multi-tasking knowledge workers. *Proceedings of the 10th international conference on Intelligent user interfaces*. DOI: 10.1145/1040830.1040855 Cited on page(s) 57, 64

Emirbayer, M. and Mische, A. (1998) What is agency? *American Journal of Sociology* 103: 962–1023. Cited on page(s) 40

Engeström, Y. (1987) *Learning by Expanding: An Activity-Theoretical Approach to Developmental Research*. Helsinki: Orienta-Konsultit Oy. Cited on page(s) 11, 33, 34, 46

Engeström, Y., Miettinen, R., and Punamäki, R. (eds.), (1999) *Perspectives on Activity Theory*. Cambridge: Cambridge University Press. Cited on page(s) 11, 32

EUSSET (2009) A position statement. European Society for Socially Embedded Technologies (EUSSET). Available at `http://www.eusset.eu/index.php?id=5` Cited on page(s) 74

Fällman, D. (2003) *In Romance with the Materials of Mobile Interaction: A Phenomenological Approach to the Design of Mobile Information Technology*. (PhD Thesis). Umeå Universitet. Cited on page(s) 50

Fischer, G., Giaccardi, E., Ye, Y., Sutcliffe, A. G., and Mehandjiev, N. (2004) Meta-design: A manifesto for end-user development. *Communications of the ACM* 47(9): 33–37. DOI: 10.1145/1015864.1015884 Cited on page(s) 73

Forlizzi, J. and Battarbee, K. (2004) Understanding experience in interactive systems. *Proc. DIS 2004*. NY: ACM. Pp. 261–268. DOI: 10.1145/1013115.1013152 Cited on page(s) 47

Forlizzi, J. (2008) The product ecology: Understanding social product use and supporting design culture. *International Journal of Design* 2(1): 11–20. Cited on page(s) 73

Freeman, E. and Gelernter, D. (2007) Beyond Lifestreams: The inevitable demise of the desktop metaphor. In V. Kaptelinin and M. Czerwinski (eds.), *Beyond the Desktop Metaphor: Designing Integrated Digital Work Environments*. Cambridge: The MIT Press. Pp. 19–48. Cited on page(s) 57

Friedman, B., Kahn, P. H., Jr., and Borning, A. (2006) Value sensitive design and information systems. In P. Zhang and D. Galletta (eds.), *Human-Computer Interaction in Management Information Systems: Foundations*. Armonk, NY, London: M. E. Sharpe. Pp. 348–372. Cited on page(s) 73

Gibson, J. J. (1979) *The Ecological Approach to Visual Perception*. Boston: Houghton Mifflin. Cited on page(s) 6

González, V., Nardi, B., and Mark, G. (2009) Ensembles: Understanding the instantiation of activities. *Information, Technology, and People*, 22:109–131. DOI: 10.1108/09593840910962195 Cited on page(s) 9

Grudin, J. (1990) The computer reaches out: The historical continuity of interface design. *Proc. CHI 1990*. NY: ACM. Pp. 261–268. Cited on page(s) 66

Hassenzahl, M. (2003) The thing and I: Understanding the relationship between user and product. In M. Blythe, C. Overbeeke, A. F. Monk, and P. C. Wright (eds.), *Funology: From Usability to Enjoyment*. Dordrecht: Kluwer. Pp. 31–42. Cited on page(s) 47

Heidegger, M. (1962) *Being and Time*. English translation 1962. New York: Harper & Row. (First published in German in 1927). Cited on page(s) 40, 51

Henderson, A. and Card, S. (1986) Rooms: The use of virtual workspaces to reduce space contention in a window-based graphical user interface. *ACM Transactions on Graphics* 5: 211–243. DOI: 10.1145/24054.24056 Cited on page(s) 56

Hollan, J., Hutchins, E. and Kirsch, D. (2000) Distributed cognition: Toward a new foundation for human-computer interaction research. *ACM TOCHI* 7: 174–196. DOI: 10.1145/353485.353487 Cited on page(s) 1, 50

Hornecker, E. and Buur, J. (2006) Getting a grip on tangible interaction: A framework on physical space and social interaction. *Proc. CHI 2006*. NY: ACM. Pp. 437–446. Cited on page(s) 51

Huang, E. M., Blevis, E., Mankoff, J., Nathan, L. P., and Tomlinson, B. (2009) Defining the role of HCI in the challenges of sustainability. *Proc. CHI EA 2009*. NY: ACM. Pp. 4827–4830. DOI: 10.1145/1520340.1520751 Cited on page(s) 67

Huizing, A. and Cavanagh, M. (2011) Planting contemporary practice theory in the garden of information science. *Information Research* 16 (4). http://informationr.net/ir/16--4/paper497.html Cited on page(s) 67, 70

Ilyenkov, E. V. (2008) *Dialectical Logic: Essays on Its History and Theory*. Aakar Books (originally published in Russian in 1974). Cited on page(s) 32

Jacob, R., Girouard, A. Hirshfield, L., Horn, M., Shaer, O., Solovey, E., and Zigelbaum, J. (2008) Reality-based interaction: A framework for post-WIMP interfaces. *Proc. CHI 2008*. NY: ACM. DOI: 10.1145/1357054.1357089 Cited on page(s) 66

Jonassen, D. and Rohrer-Murphy, L. (1999) Activity theory as a framework for designing constructivist learning environments. *Educational Technology, Research and Development* 47: 61–79. DOI: 10.1007/BF02299477 Cited on page(s) 7

Kallinikos, J. (2004) Farewell to constructivism: Technology and context-embedded action. In C. Avgerou, C. Ciborra, and F. Land (eds.), *The Social Study of Information and Communication Technology: Innovation, Actors, and Contexts*. Oxford: Oxford University Press. Pp. 140–161. Cited on page(s) 72

Kallinikos, J. (2012) Form, function and matter: Crossing the border of materiality. In P. Leonardi, B. Nardi, and J. Kallinikos, (eds.) *Materiality and Organizing: Social Interaction in a Technological World*. Oxford: Oxford University Press. Cited on page(s) 72

Kaptelinin, V. (1992) Human computer interaction in context: The activity theory perspective. *Proceedings of the 1992 East-West International Conference, EWHCI'92*. (St. Petersburg, Russia, August 1992). Pp. 7–13. Cited on page(s) 5

Kaptelinin, V. (1996a) Creating computer-based work environments: An empirical study of Macintosh users. *Proceedings of the 1996 ACM SIGCPR/SIGMIS Conference*. (Denver, Colorado, April 1996). Pp. 360–366. Cited on page(s) 55

Kaptelinin, V. (1996b) Distribution of cognition between minds and artifacts: Augmentation or mediation? *AI and Society* 10: 15–25. Cited on page(s) 28

Kaptelinin, V., Nardi, B., and Macaulay, C. (1999) The Activity Checklist: A tool for representing the "space" of context. *Interactions* 6: 27–39. Cited on page(s) 7

Kaptelinin, V., Nardi, B., Bødker, B., Carroll, J., Hollan, J., Hutchins, H., and Winograd, T. (2003) Post-cognitivist HCI: Second-wave theories. *Proc. CHI EA 2003*. DOI: 10.1145/765891.765933 Cited on page(s) 1, 46

Kaptelinin, V. (2003) UMEA: Translating interaction histories into project contexts. *Proc. CHI 2003*. NY: ACM. Pp. 353-360. DOI: 10.1145/642611.642673 Cited on page(s) 57, 60, 64

Kaptelinin, V. and Nardi, B. (2006) *Acting with technology: Activity theory and interaction design*. Cambridge: MIT Press. Cited on page(s) 5, 7, 12, 29, 37, 50, 65, 67

Kaptelinin, V. and Czerwinski, M. (2007) Introduction. In V. Kaptelinin and M. Czerwinski (eds.), *Beyond the Desktop Metaphor: Designing Integrated Digital Work Environments*. Cambridge: MIT Press. Pp. 1–12. Cited on page(s) 55, 56

Kaptelinin, V. and Bannon, L. (2012) Interaction design beyond the product: Creating technology-enhanced activity spaces. To appear in *Human Computer Interaction*. Cited on page(s) 73

Kaptelinin, V. and Nardi, B. (2012) Affordances in HCI: Toward a mediated action perspective. *Proc. CHI 2012*. NY. ACM. Cited on page(s) 5, 6

Kaptelinin, V. and Uden, L. (2012) Understanding delegated actions: Toward an activity-theoretical perspective on service design. *Proc. ServDes 2012*. (Espoo, Finland, February 2012). Cited on page(s) 5

Kirsh, D. (2001) The context of work. *Human-computer Interaction* 16: 305–322. DOI: 10.1207/S15327051HCI16234_12 Cited on page(s) 73

Klemmer, S- R., Hartman, B., and Takayama, L. (2006) How bodies matter: Five themes for interaction design. *Proc. DIS 2006*. NY: ACM. DOI: 10.1145/1142405.1142429 Cited on page(s) 51

Kuutti, K. (1991) Activity theory and its applications to information systems research and development. In H.-E. Nissen, H. K. Klein, and R. Hirschheim (eds.), *Information Systems Research Arena of the 90's*. Amsterdam: North Holland. Pp. 525–549. Cited on page(s) 5

Kuutti, K. (2010) Where are the Ionians of user experience research? *Proc. NordiCHI 2010*. NY: ACM. Pp. 715–718. DOI: 10.1145/1868914.1869012 Cited on page(s) 3, 5, 49, 50, 73

Kuutti, K. (2011) Out of the shadow of Simon: Artifacts, practices, and history in design research. *Proceedings of the Doctoral Education in Design Conference*, Hong Kong. Cited on page(s) 67, 70, 71

Latour, B. (1993) Ethnography of a 'high-tech' case: About Aramis. In P. Lemannier (ed.), *Technological Choices: Transformations in Material Culture Since the Neolithic*. London: Routledge and Kegan Paul. Pp. 372–398. Cited on page(s) 37, 41

Law, J. and M. Callon. (1992) The life and death of an aircraft. In W. Bijker and J. Law (eds.), *Shaping Technology/Building Society*. Pp. 20–52. Cambridge: MIT Press. Cited on page(s) 37

Le Dantec, C. and Edwards, W. (2008) The view from the trenches: Organization, power, and technology at two nonprofit homeless outreach centers. *Proc. CSCW 2008*. NY: ACM. Pp. 589–98. DOI: 10.1145/1460563.1460656 Cited on page(s) 68

Leonardi, P. M. and Barley, S. R. (2008) Materiality and change: Challenges to building better theory about technology and organizing. *Information and Organization* 18, 159–176. DOI: 10.1016/j.infoandorg.2008.03.001 Cited on page(s) 2

Leontiev, A. (1944) On some psychological questions of consciousness as an aspect of learning. *Soviet Pedagogy* 1944(2): 65–75. (In Russian). Cited on page(s) 48

Leontiev, A. (1975) *Activity. Consciousness. Personality.* [Dejatelnost. Soznanie. Lichnost] Moscow: Politizdat. (In Russian). Cited on page(s) 20

Leontiev, A. (1978) (Leont'ev) *Activity, Consciousness, and Personality.* Englewood Cliffs, NJ: Prentice-Hall. Cited on page(s) 11, 16, 25, 26, 27, 42, 49, 59, 74

Leontiev, A. (1979) The psychology of image. *Vestnik MGU, Seria 14. Psikhologija.* (In Russian). Cited on page(s) 49

Leontiev, A. (1981) (Leont'ev) *Problems in the Development of the Mind.* Moscow: Progress Publishers. Cited on page(s) 11, 16, 22, 28, 48, 59

Li, Y. and Landay, J. A. (2008) Activity-based prototyping of ubicomp applications for long-lived, everyday human activities. *Proc. CHI 2008.* NY: ACM. Pp. 1303–1312. DOI: 10.1145/1357054.1357259 Cited on page(s) 8

Manker, J. and Arvola, M. (2011) Prototyping in game design: Externalization and internalization of game ideas. *Proc. HCI 2011: Health, Wealth, and Happiness. The 25th BCS Conference on Human-Computer Interaction.* (Newcastle Upon Tyne, UK, July 2011). Cited on page(s) 5, 7

Mankoff, J., Matthews, D., Fussell, S. R., and Johnson, M. (2007) Leveraging social networks to motivate individuals to reduce their ecological footprints. *Proc. HICSS 2007.* IEEE Computer Society. DOI: 10.1109/HICSS.2007.325 Cited on page(s) 67

Mankoff, J., Kravets, R., and Blevis, E. (2008) Some computer science issues in creating a sustainable world. *Computer* 41(8): 102–105. DOI: 10.1109/MC.2008.307 Cited on page(s) 67

Mark, G., Bagdouri, M., Palen, L., Martin, J., Al-Ani, B., and Anderson, K. (2012) Blogs as a collective war diary. *Proc. CSCW 2012.* NY: ACM. DOI: 10.1145/2145204.2145215 Cited on page(s) 68

Maslow, A. (1968) *Toward a Psychology of Being.* New York: Wiley. Cited on page(s) 26

Matthews, T., Rattenbury, T., and Carter, S. (2007) Defining, designing, and evaluating peripheral displays: An analysis using activity theory. *Human-Computer Interaction*, 22(1-2): 221–261. Cited on page(s) 7

McCarthy, J. and Wright, P. (2004) *Technology as experience.* Cambridge: MIT Press. Cited on page(s) 47

Mescherjakov, B. and Zinchenko, V. P. (eds.), (2003) *Big Psychological Dictionary*. (In Russian). Prime-Evroznak. Cited on page(s) 14

Miettinen, R., Samra-Fredericks, D., and Yanow, D. (2009) Re-turn to practice: An introductory essay. *Organization Studies* 30(12): 1309–1327. DOI: 10.1177/0170840609349860 Cited on page(s) 74

Millen, D. R., Muller, M. J., Geyer, W., Wilcox, E., and Brownholtz, B. (2005) Patterns of media use in an activity-centric environment. *Proc. CHI 2005*. NY: ACM. Pp. 879–888. DOI: 10.1145/1054972.1055096 Cited on page(s) 58

Moran, T. (2005a) Unified Activity Management: Explicitly representing activity in work-support systems. Working paper. *ECSCW 2005 Workshop on Activity*. Cited on page(s) 11, 58, 60, 62

Moran, T. (2005b) Activity: Analysis, design, and management. In S. Bagnara and G. Crampton Smith (eds.), *Theories and Practice in Interaction Design*. Lawrence Erlbaum. Cited on page(s) 58

Moran, T., Cozzi, A., and Farrell, S. P. (2005) Unified Activity Management: Supporting people in e-business. *Communications of the ACM* 48 (12): 67–70. DOI: 10.1145/1101779.1101811 Cited on page(s) 58

Muller, M., Geyer, W., Brownholtz, B., Wilcox, E., and Millen, D. (2004) One hundred days in an activity-centric collaboration environment based on shared objects. *Proc. CHI 2004*. NY: ACM. Pp. 375–382. DOI: 10.1145/985692.985740 Cited on page(s) 58

Mwanza, D. (2002) Conceptualising work activity for CAL systems design. *Journal of Computer Assisted Learning* 18: 84–92. DOI: 10.1046/j.0266-4909.2001.00214.x Cited on page(s) 7

Nardi, B. (1992) Studying context: A comparison of activity theory, situated action models, and distributed cognition. *Proceedings of the 1992 East-West International HCI Conference, EWHCI'92*. (St. Petersburg, Russia, August 1992). Pp. 352–359. Cited on page(s) 5

Nardi, B. (1994) Studying task-specificity; or, How we could have done it right the first time with activity theory. *Proceedings of the 1994 East-West International HCI Conference, EWHCI'94*. (St. Petersburg, Russia, August 1994). Pp. 1–6. Cited on page(s) 5

Nardi, B. (1996a) Studying context. In B. Nardi (ed.), *Context and Consciousness: Activity Theory and Human-Computer Interaction*. Cambridge: MIT Press. Cited on page(s) 5, 11, 65, 73

Nardi, B. (ed.), (1996b) *Context and Consciousness: Activity Theory and Human-Computer Interaction*. Cambridge: MIT Press. Cited on page(s) 5

Nardi, B., Whittaker, S., Isaacs, E., Creech, M., Johnson, J., and Hainsworth, J. (2002) Integrating communication and information through ContactMap. *Communications of the ACM* 45(4): Pp. 89–95. DOI: 10.1145/505248.505251 Cited on page(s) 57

Nardi, B. (2005) Objects of desire: Power and passion in collaborative activity. *Mind, Culture, and Activity: An International Journal* 12: 37–51. DOI: 10.1207/s15327884mca1201_4 Cited on page(s) 5

Nardi, B., Vatrapu, R., and Clemmensen, T. (2011) Comparative Informatics. *Interactions* March. Pp. 28–33. Cited on page(s) 68

Nathan, L. (2008) Ecovillages, values, and information technology: Balancing sustainability with daily life in 21st century America. *Proc. CHI 2008*. NY: ACM. Pp. 2723–2728. Cited on page(s) 67

Nelson, H. and Stolterman, E. (2003) *The Design Way—Intentional Change in an Unpredictable World*. New Jersey: Educational Technology Publications. Cited on page(s) 49, 75

Newell, A. and Card, S. (1986) Straightening out softening up: Response to Carroll and Campbell. *Human-Computer Interaction* 2: 17. Cited on page(s) 69

Norman, D. (1991) Cognitive artifacts. In J. Carroll (ed.), *Designing Interaction: Psychology at the Human-Computer Interface*. Cambridge: Cambridge University Press. Pp. 17–38. Cited on page(s) 1, 59

Norman, D. (1998) *The Invisible Computer. Why Good Products Can Fail, the Personal Computer is so Complex, and Information Appliances are the Solution*. Cambridge: MIT Press. Cited on page(s) 56

Norman, D. (2004) *Emotional Design: Why We Love (or Hate) Everyday Things*. Basic Books. Cited on page(s) 47

Norman, D. (2005) Human-centered design considered harmful. *Interactions* 12(4): 14–19. DOI: 10.1145/1070960.1070976 Cited on page(s) 56

Norman. D. (2006) Logic versus usage: The case for activity-centered design. *Interactions* 13(6): 45. DOI: 10.1145/1167948.1167978 Cited on page(s) 56

Palen, L., Hiltz, S., and Liu, S. (2007) Online forums supporting grassroots participation in emergency preparedness and response. *Communications of the ACM* 50(3): 54–58. DOI: 10.1145/1226736.1226766 Cited on page(s) 68, 73

Patterson, D., Sim, S., and Aiyelokun, T. (2009) Overcoming blind spots in interaction design: A case study in designing for African AIDS orphan care communities. *Information Technologies & International Development* 5(4): 75–88. Cited on page(s) 68, 72, 75

Pickering, A. (1993) The mangle of practice: Agency and emergence in the sociology of science. *American Journal of Sociology* 99: 559–589. Cited on page(s) 38

Plaisant, C. and Shneiderman, B. (1994) Organization overviews and role management: Inspiration for future desktop environments. *Proc. WET-ICE '95*. DOI: 10.1109/ENABL.1995.484544 Cited on page(s) 56

Polt, R. (1999) *Heidegger: An Introduction*. London: UCL Press. Cited on page(s) 51

Postman, N. (1993) *Technopoly: The Surrender of Culture to Technology*. New York: Vintage Books. Cited on page(s) 42

Qu, Y., Wu, P. F., and Wang, X. (2009) Online community response to major disaster: A study of Tianya forum in the 2008 Sichuan earthquake. *Proc. HICSS 2009*. IEEE Computer Society. Pp. 1–11. DOI: 10.1109/HICSS.2009.330 Cited on page(s) 68

Quek, A. and Shah, H. (2004) A comparative survey of activity-based methods for information systems development. *Proceedings of the 6th International Conference on Enterprise Information Systems, ICEIS*. (Porto, Portugal, April 2004). Pp. 221–232. Cited on page(s) 7

Rabardel, P. and Bourmaud, G. (2003) From computer to instrument system: A developmental perspective. *Interacting with Computers* 15: 665–691. DOI: 10.1016/S0953-5438(03)00058-4 Cited on page(s) 32, 36

Reynolds, C. (1987) Flocks, herds, and schools: A distributed behavioral model. *Computer Graphics* 21: 25–34. Cited on page(s) 42

Robertson, G., van Dantzich, M., Robbins, D., Czerwinski, M., Hinckley, K., Risden, K., Thiel, D., and Gorokhovsky, V. (2000) The Task Gallery: A 3D window manager. *Proc. CHI 2000*. NY: ACM. Pp. 494–501. DOI: 10.1145/332040.332482 Cited on page(s) 56

Robertson, G., Smith, G., Meyers, B., Baudisch, P., Czerwinski, M., Horvitz, E., Robbins, D., and Tan, D. (2007) Explorations in task management on the desktop. In V. Kaptelinin and M. Czerwinski (eds.), *Beyond the Desktop Metaphor: Designing Integrated Digital Work Environments*. Cambridge: The MIT Press. Pp. 101–138. Cited on page(s) 58, 63

Robinson, M. (1980) *Housekeeping*. New York: Farrar, Straus, and Giroux. Cited on page(s) 40

Rogers, Y. (2004) New theoretical approaches for HCI. *Annual Review of Information Science and Technology* 38: 87–143. DOI: 10.1002/aris.1440380103 Cited on page(s) 9

Rose, J., Jones, M., and Truex, D. (2005) Socio-theoretic accounts of IS: The problem of agency. *Scandinavian Journal of Information Systems* 17: 133–152. Cited on page(s) 38

Rubinshtein, S. L. (1946) *Foundations of General Psychology*. Second edition. [Osnovy Obschej Psikhologii. 2-e izdanie]. Moscow: Uchpedgiz. (In Russian). Cited on page(s) 14, 19, 45, 48

Rubinshtein, S. L. (1986) The principle of creative self-activity (on the philosophical foundations of modern pedagogy). Originally published in 1922. *Voprosy Psikhologii* 4: 101–107. (In Russian). Cited on page(s) 12

Sambasivan, N., Cutrell, E., Toyama, K., and Nardi, B. (2010) Intermediated technology use in developing communities. *Proc. CHI 2010*. NY: ACM. Pp. 2583–2592. DOI: 10.1145/1753326.1753718 Cited on page(s) 68

Shaffer, D. and Clinton, K. (2006) Toolforthoughts: Reexamining thinking in the digital age. *Mind, Culture, and Activity* 13: 283–300. Cited on page(s) 42

Shklovski, I., Burke, M., Kiesler, S., and Kraut, R. (2010) Technology adoption and use in the aftermath of Hurricane Katrina in New Orleans. *American Behavioral Scientist* 53(8): 1228–1246. DOI: 10.1177/0002764209356252 Cited on page(s) 68

Sousa, J. P. and Garlan, D. (2001) From computers everywhere to tasks anywhere: The Aura approach. Available at `http://www.cs.cmu.edu/~aura/docdir/sg01.pdf` Cited on page(s) 58

Spinuzzi, C. (2003) *Tracing genres through organizations: A sociocultural approach to information design*. Cambridge: The MIT Press. Cited on page(s) 36, 73

Spinuzzi, C. (2011). Losing by expanding: Corralling the runaway object. *Journal of Business and Technical Communication* 25(4), 449–486. Cited on page(s) 35

Stahl, G. (2011) Theories of cognition in CSCW. In S. Bødker, N. O. Bouvin, V. Wulf, L. Ciolfi, and W. Lutters (eds.), *ECSCW 2011: Proceedings of the 12th European Conference on Computer Supported Cooperative Work, 24-28 September 2011, Aarhus Denmark*. Springer. Cited on page(s) 9

Starbird, K. and Palen, L. (2011) Voluntweeters: Self-organizing by digital volunteers in times of crisis. *Proc. CHI 2011*. NY: ACM. Pp. 1071–1080. DOI: 10.1145/1978942.1979102 Cited on page(s) 68

Stetsenko. A. (2008) From relational ontology to transformative activist stance on development and learning: Expanding Vygotsky's (CHAT) project. *Cultural Studies of Science Education* 3: 471–491. DOI: 10.1007/s11422-008-9111-3 Cited on page(s) 3, 4, 65, 66, 70, 76

Suchman, L. (1987) *Plans and Situated Actions*. Cambridge: Cambridge University Press. Cited on page(s) 1

Svanaes, D. (2000) *Understanding Interactivity: Steps to a Phenomenology of Human-Computer Interaction*. Trondheim, Norway, Norges Teknisk-Naturvitenskapelige Universitet (NTNU). Cited on page(s) 50, 52

Tainter, J. (1990) *The Collapse of Complex Societies*. Cambridge University Press. Cited on page(s) 67, 68

Tainter, J. (2006) Social complexity and sustainability. *Ecological Complexity* 3(2): 91–103. DOI: 10.1016/j.ecocom.2005.07.004 Cited on page(s) 67, 68

Tenner, E. (1997) *Why Things Bite Back: Technology and the Revenge of Unintended Consequences*. New York: Vintage Books. Cited on page(s) 42

Tomlinson, B. (2010) *Greening through IT: Information Technology for Environmental Sustainability*. Cambridge: MIT Press. Cited on page(s) 67

Tomlinson, B., Silberman, S., Patterson, D., Pan, Y. and Blevis, E. (2012) Collapse informatics: Augmenting the sustainability & ICT4D discourse in HCI. *Proc. CHI EA 2012*. NY: ACM. Cited on page(s) 65, 67, 68

Torrey, C., Burke, M., Lee, M., Dey, A., Fussell, S., and Kiesler, S. (2007) Connected giving: Ordinary people coordinating disaster relief on the Internet. *Proc. HICSS 20007*. IEEE Computer Society. DOI: 10.1109/HICSS.2007.144 Cited on page(s) 68

Toyama, K. (2010) *Human-Computer Interaction and Global Development*. Now Publishers Inc. Cited on page(s) 68

Uden, L. (2007) Activity theory for designing mobile learning. *Int. J. Mobile Learning and Organization* 1(1): 81–102. DOI: 10.1504/IJMLO.2007.011190 Cited on page(s) 5

Unified   Activity   Management   (n.d.)
http://domino.research.ibm.com/comm/research
_projects.nsf/pages/uam.index.html Cited on page(s) 58

Vardi, M. Y. (2009) The financial meltdown and computing. *Communications of the ACM* 52(5). DOI: 10.1145/1562164.1562165 Cited on page(s) 67, 68

Voida, S., Mynatt, E., MacIntyre, B., and Corso G. (2002) Integrating virtual and physical context to support knowledge workers. *IEEE Pervasive Computing* 1: 73–79.
DOI: 10.1109/MPRV.2002.1037725 Cited on page(s) 56, 59

Voida, S., Mynatt, E., and MacIntyre, B. (2007) Supporting activity in desktop and ubiquitous computing. In V. Kaptelinin and M. Czerwinski (eds.), *Beyond the Desktop Metaphor: Designing Integrated Digital Work Environments*. Cambridge: MIT Press. Pp. 195–222. Cited on page(s) 56, 59

Voida, S., Mynatt, E. D, and Edwards, W. K. (2008) Re-framing the desktop interface around the activities of knowledge work. *Proc. UIST 2008*. NY: ACM. DOI: 10.1145/1449715.1449751 Cited on page(s) 59

Voida, S. and Mynatt, E. (2009) It feels better than filing: Everyday work experiences in an activity-based computing system. *Proc. CHI 2009*. NY: ACM. DOI: 10.1145/1518701.1518744 Cited on page(s) 57, 59, 64

Vygotsky, L. S. (1962) *Thought and Language*. Cambridge: MIT Press. DOI: 10.1037/11193-000 Cited on page(s) 75

Vygotsky, L. S. (1978) *Mind in Society: The Development of Higher Psychological Processes*. Cambridge: Harvard University Press. Cited on page(s) 14, 47, 75

Vygotsky, L. S. (1982) Instrumental method in psychology [Instrumentalnyj metod v psikhologii]. In A. Luria and M. Yaroshevsky (eds.), *L. S. Vygotsky. Collected Works*. V. 1. [L. S. Vygotsky. Sobranie Sochinenij. T. 1]. Moscow: Pedagogika. Pp. 103–109, (in Russian). Cited on page(s) 15, 16, 17

Vygotsky, L. S. (1983) The history of the development of higher psychological functions [Istorija razvitija vysshyh psikhicheskih funktsij]. In A. Matyushkin (ed.), *L. S. Vygotsky. Collected Works*. V. 3. [L. S. Vygotsky. Sobranie Sochinenij. T. 3]. Moscow: Pedagogika. Pp. 5–328, (in Russian). Cited on page(s) 15, 16, 47

Wenix Hvor er det latterligt at indfører sådan noget. (2003) `http://newz.dk/ae-oe-og-aa-i-com-net-org-domaener`. Cited on page(s) 72

Wertsch J. (1981) The concept of activity in Soviet psychology: An introduction. In J. Wertsch (ed.), *The Concept of Activity in Soviet Psychology*. Armonk, New York: M.E. Sharpe. Pp. 3–36. Cited on page(s) 29

Wertsch, J. (1998) *Mind as Action*. New York: Oxford University Press. Cited on page(s) 41, 46

Wilson, T. (2008) Activity theory and information seeking. *Annual Review of Information Science and Technology* 42(1): 119–161. DOI: 10.1002/aris.2008.1440420111 Cited on page(s) 5

Windows Managers for X: The basics (n.d.). `http://xwinman.org/basics.php/` Cited on page(s) 56

Winner, L. (1977) *Autonomous Technology: Technic Out of Control as a Theme in Political Thought*. Cambridge: MIT Press. Cited on page(s) 42

Winner, L. (1986) *The Whale and the Reactor: A Search for Limits in an Age of High Technology*. Chicago: University of Chicago Press. Cited on page(s) 42

Winograd, T. and Flores, F. (1987) *Understanding computers and cognition*. Addison-Wesley. Cited on page(s) 1

Woelfer, J., Iverson, A., Hendry, D., Friedman, B., and Gill, B. (2011) Improving the safety of homeless young people with mobile phones: Values, form and function. *Proc. CHI 2011*. NY: ACM. Pp. 1707–1716. DOI: 10.1145/1978942.1979191 Cited on page(s) 68

Wong, J. (2009) Prepare for descent: Interaction design. In *Our New Future. Defining the Role of HCI in the Challenges of Sustainability, Workshop at CHI 2009*. Cited on page(s) 68, 73

Zinchenko, V. (1996) Developing activity theory: The zone of proximal development and beyond. In B. Nardi (ed.), *Context and Consciousness: Activity Theory and Human-Computer Interaction*. Cambridge: MIT Press. Pp. 283–324. Cited on page(s) 28, 41

Authors' Biographies

VICTOR KAPTELININ

Victor Kaptelinin is a Professor at the Department of Information Science and Media Studies, University of Bergen, Norway, and the Department of Informatics, Umeå University, Sweden. He has held teaching and/or research positions at the Psychological Institute of Russian Academy of Education, Moscow Lomonosov University, and University of California, San Diego, USA. His main research interests are in interaction design, activity theory, and educational use of information technologies.

BONNIE NARDI

Bonnie Nardi is an anthropologist in the Department of Informatics at the University of California, Irvine. She is interested in social life on the Internet and works with activity theory as her principal orientation. Bonnie's recent book on virtual worlds, *My Life as a Night Elf Priest: An Anthropological Account of World of Warcraft*, was published by the University of Michigan Press in 2010. A forthcoming book *Ethnography and Virtual Worlds: A Handbook of Method* (with T. Boellstorff, C. Pearce. and T.L. Taylor) will be published in August 2012 by Princeton University Press.

Printed in the United States
by Baker & Taylor Publisher Services